THE PLAN OF SALVATION

THE PLAN OF SALVATION

by

BENJAMIN B. WARFIELD

Professor of Didactic and Polemic Theology
Princeton Theological Seminary
1887-1921

SIMPSON
PUBLISHING COMPANY

Simpson Publishing Company
1 South Main Street
Post Office Box 100
Avinger, Texas 75630
U.S.A.

First Edition published by Presbyterian Board of Publication 1915
Second Edition published by Presbyterian Board of Publication 1918
Revised Edition published by Wm. B. Eerdmans Publishing Company 1935

Printed in the United States of America
by BookMasters, Inc.
Ashland, Ohio

ISBN 0-9622508-0-5

To

JOHN DeWITT, D.D., LL.D.

EMERITUS PROFESSOR OF CHURCH HISTORY IN
PRINCETON SEMINARY

Lover of Letters
Lover of Men
Lover of God

Contents

Foreword

These lectures by Dr. Benjamin B. Warfield offer a lucid and penetrating analysis of God's plan of salvation from sin. They form a valuable companion to a systematic study of the scriptural witness to God's plan of salvation.

In this book Dr. Warfield identifies the crucial questions associated with God's plan of salvation. He gives a shattering critique of the most dangerous answers that men have devised to those questions. He also exposes the injury to men's souls and the affront to God's glory which must necessarily result from those errors. Herein lies the enduring value of this work.

The reader will note, however, the pungent smell of the battlefield of dogmatics, rather than the sweet aroma of fresh exposition of the Scriptures. This limitation should neither offend nor discourage the reader. Since this book was not intended to be an expository work, the reader should not expect it to stand alone as a polemic for the Reformed faith, as though our faith should stand upon the reasoning of godly men rather than upon the exposition of the word of God.

Originally the substance of this book was delivered in 1914 as five theological lectures at the Princeton Summer School of

Theology. Accordingly, it is laden with the technical terminology of a theological classroom, rather than presented in the everyday language of God's people. Therefore, in the following paragraphs, an explanation of the major terminology employed and a summary of the content and development of the book are offered.

Dr. Warfield observes that among those who profess adherence to Christianity the deepest cleft respecting God's plan of salvation concerns *the Author of salvation.* Supernaturalists, as the name suggests, rightly attribute the power decisive in man's salvation to God. Naturalists, on the other hand, erroneously imagine that the power essential to save man is natively his own. Dr. Warfield appropriately calls this naturalistic scheme "Autosoterism," or self-salvation.

Narrowing his scope further Warfield observes that among Supernaturalists the deepest cleft concerns *God's method of salvation.* Evangelicals (a term derived from "the evangel" or gospel) rightly confess that God saves men individually through the indispensable instrument of their personal faith in the gospel of Jesus Christ. Sacramentalists (or, as Dr. Warfield dubs them, "Sacerdotalists"), on the other hand, maintain that God saves men through the church by power vested in the sacraments, especially baptism and the mass, which they suppose automatically convey God's grace to all who receive them.

When he has thus exposed the damning errors, or heresies, of Autosoterism and Sacerdotalism, Dr. Warfield narrows his scope again, focusing next upon Evangelicalism. Among Evangelicals the deepest cleft concerns the intended *objects of salvation.* Universalists, as the name implies, wrongly maintain that everything God does with a view to saving men he does *for* and *to* all men alike. Thus they suppose that Christ died *for* all men alike to make their salvation possible and that the Holy Spirit gives *to* all men alike power sufficient to enable them to believe the gospel and be saved. Particularists also confess that men are indiscriminately called by the gospel to faith in Christ. However, in contrast to universalists, they correctly maintain that the determinative act in the salvation of a sinner is wrought by God, at his sole discretion, exclusively upon some *particular men*, God's elect, and not upon all men alike. Thus the name "Particularist" is used to describe those who hold this distinctive.

Dispensing with the serious error of Universalism, Dr. Warfield narrows his focus one final time. He observes that even among Particularists, the universalist error has a remnant in Amyraldianism. Amyraldians are named for Moses Amyraut, a seventeenth-century teacher in the theological school at Saumur, France, who is credited with inventing this scheme. They admit that God, at his sole discretion, applies salvation, through the regenerating work of the Holy Spirit, exclusively to God's elect; but then they imagine, wrongly and inconsistently, that Christ died for all men alike to make their salvation possible, thus succumbing at last to universalism.

Calvinism alone, Dr. Warfield concludes, manifests consistent particularism. The distinctives of Calvinism were first articulated comprehensively in the pronouncements of the Reformed Synod of Dort in 1619, which are better known as "the five points of Calvinism." Calvinists confess unashamedly that Christ died exclusively *for* God's elect to accomplish their salvation and that the Holy Spirit applies salvation exclusively *to* God's elect, by regenerating them and creating faith in Christ in their hearts.

In Calvinism then, and in Calvinism alone, Dr. Warfield finds a conception of God's plan of salvation which, being true to Scripture, ascribes all the glory to God, and to God alone. May the republication of these lectures contribute to that great end. To God alone be all the glory for the salvation of his people from their sins.

GREGORY G. NICHOLS

Pastor, Trinity Baptist Church

Professor of Systematic Theology,
Trinity Ministerial Academy

Montville, New Jersey
March 8, 1989

Preface to the Present Edition

Most of Dr. Warfield's writings have been reprinted in recent years and are presently available. *The Plan of Salvation*, however, is not included in any of these editions and has been out of print for many years. Thus, it is a delight to make these classic lectures available again and to complement the existing works of Dr. Warfield now in print.

This edition includes the notes and corrections which were made by Dr. Warfield before his death. A previously published Revised Edition, however, omitted the quotations of Scripture which were cited at the beginning of each lecture. These references are included in this edition as they were in the First and Second Editions and the 1935 Revised Edition.

THE PUBLISHER

THE PLAN OF SALVATION

Lecture 1

The Differing Conceptions

Of him are ye in Christ Jesus.

—1 Corinthians 1:30

The Differing Conceptions

THE SUBJECT to which our attention is to be directed in this series of lectures is ordinarily spoken of as "The Plan of Salvation." Its more technical designation is, "The Order of Decrees." And this technical designation has the advantage over the more popular one, of more accurately defining the scope of the subject matter. This is not commonly confined to the process of salvation itself, but is generally made to include the entire course of the divine dealing with man which ends in his salvation. Creation is not uncommonly comprehended in it, and of course the fall, and the condition of man brought about by the fall. This portion of the subject matter may, however, certainly with some propriety, be looked upon as rather of the nature of a presupposition, than as a substantive part of the subject matter itself; and no great harm will be done if we abide by the more popular designation. Its greater concreteness gives it an advantage which should not be accounted small; and above all it has the merit of throwing into emphasis the main matter, salvation. The series of the divine activities which are brought into consideration are in any event supposed to circle around as their center, and to have as their proximate goal, the salvation of sinful man.

When the implications of this are fairly considered it may not seem to require much argument to justify the designation of the whole by the term, "The Plan of Salvation."

It does not seem necessary to pause to discuss the previous question whether God, in his saving activities, acts upon a plan. That God acts upon a plan in all his activities, is already given in Theism. On the establishment of a personal God, this question is closed. For person means purpose: precisely what distinguishes a person from a thing is that its modes of action are purposive, that all it does is directed to an end and proceeds through the choice of means to that end. Even the Deist, therefore, must allow that God has a plan. We may, no doubt, imagine an extreme form of Deism, in which it may be contended that God does not concern himself at all with what happens in his universe; that, having created it, he turns aside from it and lets it run its own course to any end that may happen to it, without having himself given a thought to it. It is needless to say, however, that no such extreme form of Deism actually exists, though, strange to say, there are some, as we shall have occasion to observe, who appear to think that in the particular matter of the salvation of man God does act much after this irresponsible fashion.

What the actual Deist stands for is law. He conceives that God commits his universe, not to unforeseen and unprepared caprice, but to law; law which God has impressed on his universe and to the guidance of which he can safely leave his universe. That is to say, even the Deist conceives God to have a plan; a plan which embraces all that happens in the universe. He differs with the Theist only as to the modes of activity by which he conceives God to carry out this plan. Deism involves a mechanical conception of the universe. God has made a machine, and just because it is a good machine, he can leave it to work out, not its, but his ends. So we may make a clock and then, just because it is a good clock, leave it to tick off the seconds, and point out the minutes, and strike the hours, and mark off the days of the month, and turn up the phases of the moon and the accompanying tides; and if we choose, we may put in a comet which shall appear on the dial but once in the life of the clock, not erratically, but when and where and how we have arranged for it to appear. The clock does not go its own way; it goes our way, the way which we have arranged for it to go; and God's clock, the universe, goes not its way but his way, as he has ordained for it, grinding out the inevitable events with mechanical precision.

This is a great conception, the Deist conception of law. It delivers us from chance. But it does so, only to cast us into the cogged teeth of a machine. It is, therefore, not the greatest conception. The greatest conception is the conception of Theism, which delivers us even from law, and places us in the immediate hands of a person. It is a great thing to be delivered from the inordinate realm of aimless chance. The goddess Tyche, Fortuna, was one of the most terrible divinities of the old world, quite as terrible as and scarcely distinguishable from Fate. It is a great thing to be under the control of intelligent purpose. But it makes every difference whether the purpose is executed by mere law, acting automatically, or by the ever-present personal control of the person himself. There is nothing more ordinate than the control of a person, all of whose actions are governed by intelligent purpose, directed to an end.

If we believe in a personal God, then, and much more if, being Theists, we believe in the immediate control by this personal God of the world he has made, we must believe in a plan underlying all that God does, and therefore also in a plan of salvation. The only question that can arise concerns not the reality but the nature of this plan. As to its nature, however, it must be admitted that a great many differing opinions have been held. Indeed pretty nearly every possible opinion has been announced at one time or another, in one quarter or another. Even if we leave all extra-Christian opinions to one side, we need scarcely modify this statement. Lines of division have been drawn through the Church; parties have been set over against parties; and different types of belief have been developed which amount to nothing less than different systems of religion, which are at one in little more than the mere common name of Christian, claimed by them all.

It is my purpose in this lecture to bring before us in a rapid survey such of these varying views as have been held by large parties in the Church, that some conception may be formed of their range and relations. This may be most conveniently done by observing, in the first instance at least, only the great points of difference which separate them. I shall enumerate them in the order of significance, proceeding from the most profound and far-reaching differences which divide Christians to those of less radical effect.

1. The deepest cleft which separates men calling themselves Christians in their conceptions of the plan of salvation, is that which divides what we may call the Naturalistic and the Supernaturalistic views. The line of division here is whether, in the matter of the salvation of man, God has planned simply to leave men, with more or less completeness, to save themselves, or whether he has planned himself to intervene to save them. The issue between the naturalist and the supernaturalist is thus the eminently simple but quite absolute one: Does man save himself or does God save him?

The consistently naturalistic scheme is known in the history of doctrine as Pelagianism. Pelagianism in its purity, affirms that all the power exerted in saving man is native to man himself. But Pelagianism is not merely a matter of history, nor does it always exist in its purity. As the poor in earthly goods are always with us, so the poor in spiritual things are also always with us. It may indeed be thought that there never was a period in the history of the Church in which naturalistic conceptions of the process of salvation were more wide-spread or more radical than at present. A Pelagianism which out-pelagianizes Pelagus himself in the completeness of its natural-ism is in fact at the moment intensely fashionable among the self-constituted leaders of Christian thought. And everywhere, in all communions alike, conceptions are current which assign to man, in the use of his native powers at least the decisive activity in the saving of the soul, that is to say, which suppose that God has planned that those shall be saved, who, at the decisive point, in one way or another save themselves.

These so-called intermediate views are obviously, in princi-ple, naturalistic views, since (whatever part they permit God to play in the circumstantials of salvation) when they come to the crucial point of salvation itself they cast man back upon his native powers. In so doing they separate themselves definitely from the supernaturalistic view of the plan of salvation and, with it, from the united testimony of the entire organized Church. For, however much naturalistic views have seeped into the membership of the churches, the entire organized Church—Orthodox Greek, Roman Catholic Latin, and Protestant in all its great historical forms, Lutheran and Reformed, Calvinistic and Arminian—bears its consentient, firm and emphatic testimony to the supernaturalistic conception of salvation. We shall have to journey to the periphery of Christendom, to such sects of doubtful standing in the Chris-tian body as, say, the Unitarians, to find an organized body of Christians with aught but a supernaturalistic confession.

This confession, in direct opposition to naturalism, declares with emphasis that it is God the Lord and not man himself who saves the soul; and, that no mistake may be made, it does not shrink from the complete assertion and affirms, with full understanding of the issue, precisely that all the power exerted in saving the soul is from God. Here, then, is the knife-edge which separates the two parties. The supernaturalist is not content to say that some of the power which is exerted in saving the soul; that most of the power that is exerted in saving the soul, is from God. He asserts that all the power that is exerted in saving the soul is from God, that whatever part man plays in the saving process is subsidiary, is itself the effect of the divine operation and that it is God and God alone who saves the soul. And the supernaturalist in this sense is the entire organized Church in the whole stretch of its official testimony.

2. There exist, no doubt, differences among the Supernaturalists, and differences which are not small or unimportant. The most deeply cutting of these separates the Sacerdotalists and the Evangelicals. Both sacerdotalists and evangelicals are supernaturalists. That is to say, they agree that all the power exerted in saving the soul is from God. They differ in their conception of the manner in which the power of God, by which salvation is wrought, is brought to bear on the soul. The exact point of difference between them turns on the question whether God, by whose power alone salvation is wrought, saves men by dealing himself immediately with them as individuals, or only by establishing supernatural endowed instrumentalities in the world by means of which men may be saved. The issue concerns the immediacy of the saving operations of God: Does God save men by immediate operations of his grace upon their souls, or does he act upon them only through the medium of instrumentalities established for that purpose?

The typical form of sacerdotalism is supplied by the teaching of the Church of Rome. In that teaching the church is held to be the institution of salvation, through which alone is salvation conveyed to men. Outside the church and its ordinances salvation is not supposed to be found; grace is communicated by and through the ministrations of the church, otherwise not. The two maxims are therefore in force: Where the church is, there is the Spirit; outside the church there is no salvation. The sacerdotal principle is present, however, wherever instrumentalities through which saving grace is brought to the soul are made indispensable to salvation; and it is dominant wherever this indispensability is made absolute. Thus what are called the Means of Grace are given the "necessity of means," and are made in the strict sense not merely the *sine quibus non,* but the actual *quibus* of salvation.

Over against this whole view evangelicalism, seeking to conserve what it conceives to be only consistent supernaturalism, sweeps away every intermediary between the soul and its God, and leaves the soul dependent for its salvation on God alone, operating upon it by his immediate grace. It is directly upon God and not the means of grace that the evangelical feels dependent for salvation; it is directly to God rather than to the means of grace that he looks for grace; and he proclaims the Holy Spirit therefore not only able to act but actually operative where and when and how he will. The Church and its ordinances he conceives rather as instruments which the Spirit uses than as agents which employ the Holy Spirit in working salvation. In direct opposition to the maxims of consistent sacerdotalism, he takes therefore as his mottoes: Where the Spirit is, there is the church; outside the body of the saints there is no salvation.

In thus describing evangelicalism, it will not escape notice that we are also describing Protestantism. In point of fact the whole body of Confessional Protestantism is evangelical in its view of the plan of salvation, inclusive alike of its Lutheran and Reformed, of its Calvinistic and Arminian branches. Protestantism and evangelicalism are accordingly conterminous, if not exactly synonymous designation.   As all organized Christianity is clear and emphatic in its confession of a pure supernaturalism, so all organized Protestantism is equally clear and emphatic in its confession of evangelicalism. Evangelicalism thus comes before us as the distinctively Protestant conception of the plan of salvation, and perhaps it is not strange that, in its immediate contradiction of sacerdotalism, the more deeply lying contradiction to naturalism which it equally and indeed primarily embodies is sometimes almost lost sight of.   Evangelicalism does not cease to be fundamentally antinaturalistic, however, in becoming antisacerdotal: its primary protest continues to be against naturalism, and in opposing sacerdotalism also it only is the more consistently supernaturalistic, refusing to admit any intermediaries between the soul and God, as the sole source of salvation.   That only is true evangelicalism, therefore, in which sounds clearly the double confession that all the power exerted in saving the soul is from God, and that God in his saving operations acts directly upon the soul.

3. Even so, however, there remain differences, many and deep-reaching, which divide Evangelicals among themselves. All evangelicals are agreed that all the power exerted in salvation is from God, and that God works directly upon the soul in his saving operations.   But upon the exact methods employed by God in bringing many sons into glory they differ much from one another. Some evangelicals have attained their evangelical position by a process of modification, in the way of correction, applied to a fundamental sacerdotalism, from which they have thus won their way out. Naturally elements

of this underlying sacerdotalism have remained imbedded in their construction, and color their whole mode of conceiving evangelicalism.   There are other evangelicals whose conceptions are similarly colored by an underlying naturalism, out of which they have formed their better confession by a like process of modification and correction.   The former of these parties is represented by the evangelical Lutherans, who, accordingly delight to speak of themselves as adherents of a "conservative Reformation"; that is to say, as having formed their evangelicalism on the basis of the sacerdotalism of the Church of Rome, out of which they have, painfully perhaps, though not always perfectly, made their way.   The other party is represented by the evangelical Arminians, whose evangelicalism is a correction in the interest of evangelical feeling of the underlying semi-pelagianism of the Dutch Remonstrants.   Over against all such forms there are still other evangelicals whose evangelicalism is more the pure expression of the fundamental evangelical principle, uncolored by intruding elements from without.

Amid this variety of types it is not easy to fix upon a principle of classification which will enable us to discriminate between the chief forms which evangelicalism takes by a clear line of demarkation.   Such a principle, however, seems to be provided by the opposition between what we may call the Universalistic and the Particularistic conceptions of the plan of salvation.   All evangelicals agree that all the power exerted in saving the soul is from God, and that this saving power is exerted immediately upon the soul.   But they differ as to whether God exerts this saving power equally, or at least indiscriminately, upon all men, be they actually saved or not, or rather only upon particular men, namely upon those who are actually saved.   The point of division here is whether God is conceived to have planned actually himself to save men by his almighty and certainly efficacious grace, or only so to pour out his grace upon men as to enable them to be saved, without actually securing, however, in any particular cases that they shall be saved.

The specific contention of those whom I have spoken of as universalistic is that, while all the power exerted in saving the soul is from God, and this power is exerted immediately from God upon the soul, yet all that God does, looking to the salvation of men, he does for and to all men alike, without discrimination. On the face of it this looks as if it must result in a doctrine of universal salvation. If it is God the Lord who saves the soul, and not man himself; and if God the Lord saves the soul by working directly upon it in his saving grace; and then if God the Lord so works in his saving grace upon all souls alike; it would surely seem inevitably to follow that therefore all are saved. Accordingly, there have sometimes appeared earnest evangelicals who have vigorously contended precisely on these grounds that all men are saved: salvation is wholly from God, and God is almighty, and as God works salvation by his almighty grace in all men, all men are saved. From this consistent universalism, however, the great mass of evangelical universalists have always drawn back, compelled by the clearness and emphasis of the Scriptural declaration that, in point of fact, all men are not saved. They have found themselves therefore face to face with a great problem; and various efforts have been made by them to construe the activities of God looking to salvation as all universalistic and the issue as nevertheless particularistic; while yet the fundamental evangelical principle is preserved that it is the grace of God alone which saves the soul. These efforts have given us especially the two great schemes of evangelical Lutheranism and evangelical Arminianism, the characteristic contention of both of which is that all salvation is in the hands of God alone, and all that

God does, looking to salvation, is directed indiscriminately to all men, and yet not all but some men only are saved.

Over against this inconsistent universalism, other evangelicals contend that the particularism which attaches to the issue of the saving process, must, just because it is God and God alone who saves, belong also to the process itself. In the interests of their common evangelicalism, in the interests also of the underlying supernaturalism common to all Christians, neither of which comes to its rights otherwise—nay, in the interests of religion itself—they plead that God deals throughout the whole process of salvation not with men in the mass but with individual men one by one, upon each of whom he lays hold with his grace, and each of whom he by his grace brings to salvation. As it is he who saves men, and as he saves them by immediate operations on their hearts, and as his saving grace is his almighty power effecting salvation, men owe in each and every case their actual salvation, and not merely their general opportunity to be saved, to him. And therefore, to him and to him alone belongs in each instance all the glory, which none can share with him. Thus, they contend, in order that the right evangelical ascription, *Soli Deo gloria,* may be true and suffer no diminution in meaning or in force, it is necessary to understand that it is of God that each one who is saved has everything that enters into salvation and, most of all, the very fact that it is he who enters into salvation. The precise issue which divides the universalists and the particularists is, accordingly, just whether the saving grace of God, in which alone is salvation, actually saves. Does its presence mean salvation, or may it be present, and yet salvation fail?

4. Even the Particularists, however, have their differences. The most important of these differences divides between those who hold that God has in view not all but some men, namely

those who are actually saved, in all his operations looking toward the salvation of men; and those who wish to discriminate among God's operations in this matter and to assign only to some of them a particularistic which they assign to others a universalistic reference.   The latter view is, of course, an attempt to mediate between the particularistic and the universalistic conceptions, preserving particularism in the processes as well as in the issue of salvation sufficiently to hang salvation upon the grace of God alone and to give to him all the glory of the actual salvation; while yet yielding to universalism so much of the process of salvation as its adherents think can be made at all consistent with this fundamental particularism.

The special one of the saving operations which is yielded by them to universalism is the redemption of the sinner by Christ.   This is supposed to have in the plan of God, not indeed an absolute, but a hypothetical reference to all men. All men are redeemed by Christ—that is, if they believe in him.   Their believing in him is, however, dependent on the working of faith in their hearts by God, the Holy Spirit, in his saving operations designed to give effect to the redemption of Christ.   The scheme is therefore known not merely by the name of its author, as Amyraldianism, but also, more descriptively, as Hypothetical Redemptionism, or, more commonly, as Hypothetical Universalism.   It transfers the question which divides the particularist and the universalist with respect to the plan of salvation as a whole, to the more specific question of the reference of the redeeming work of Christ.   And the precise point at issue comes therefore to be whether the redemptive work of Christ actually saves those for whom it is wrought, or only opens a possibility of salvation to them.   The hypothetical universalist, holding that its reference is to all men indifferently and that not all men are saved, cannot ascribe to it a specifically saving operation and are therefore accustomed to speak of it as rendering salvation possible to all, as opening the way of salvation to men, as removing all the obstacles to the salvation of men, or in some other similar way. On the other hand, the consistent particularist is able to look upon the redemption wrought by Christ as actually redemptive, and insists that it is in itself a saving act which actually saves, securing the salvation of those for whom it is wrought.

The debate comes thus to turn upon the nature of the redemptive work of Christ; and the particularists are able to make it very clear that whatever is added to it extensively is taken from it intensively. In other words, the issue remains here the same as in the debate with the general universalism of the Lutheran and the Arminian, namely, whether the saving operations of God actually save; though this issue is here concentrated upon a single one of these saving operations. If the saving operations of God actually save, then all those upon whom he savingly operates are saved, and particularism is given in the very nature of the case; unless we are prepared to go the whole way with universalism and declare that all men are saved. It is thus in the interests of the fundamental supernaturalistic postulate by which all organized Christianity separates itself from mere naturalism, that all the power exerted in saving the soul is from God—and of the great evangelical ascription, of *Soli Deo gloria,* as well—that the consistent particularist contends that the reference of the redemption of Christ cannot be extended beyond the body of those who are actually saved, but must be held to be only one of the operations by which God saves those whom he saves, and not they themselves. Not only, then, they contend, must we give a place to particularism in the process as well as in the issue of salvation, but a place must be vindicated for it in all the processes of salvation alike. It is God the Lord who saves; and in all the operations by which he works salvation alike, he operates for and upon, not all men indifferently, but some men only, those namely whom he saves. Thus only can we preserve to him his glory and ascribe to him and to him only the whole work of salvation.

5. The differences which have been enumerated exhaust the possibilities of differences of large moment within the limits of the plan of salvation. Men must be either Naturalists or Supernaturalists; Supernaturalists either Sacerdotalists or Evangelicals; Evangelicals either Universalistic or Particularistic; Particularists must be particularistic with respect to only some or with respect to all of God's saving operations. But the consistent particularists themselves find it still possible to differ among themselves, not indeed upon the terms of the plan of salvation itself, upon which they are all at one, but in the region of the presuppositions of that plan; and for the sake of completeness of enumeration it is desirable that this difference, too, should be adverted to here. It does not concern what God has done in the course of his saving operations; but passing behind the matter of salvation, it asks how God had dealt in general with the human race, as a race, with respect to its destiny. The two parties here are known in the history of thought by the contrasting names of Supralapsarians and Sublapsarians or Infralapsarians. The point of difference between them is whether God, in his dealing with men with reference to their destiny, divides them into two classes merely as men, or as sinners. That is to say, whether God's decree of election and preterition concerns men contemplated merely as men, or contemplated as already sinful men, a *massa corrupta.*

The mere putting of the question seems to carry its answer with it. For the actual dealing with men which is in question, is, with respect to both classes alike, those who are elected and those who are passed by, conditioned on sin: we cannot speak of salvation any more than of reprobation without positing sin. Sin is necessarily precedent in thought, not indeed to the abstract idea of discrimination, but to the concrete instance of discrimination which is in question, a discrimination with regard to a destiny which involves either salvation or punishment. There must be sin in contemplation to ground a decree of salvation, as truly a decree of punishment. We cannot speak of a decree discriminating between men with reference to salvation and punishment, therefore, without positing the contemplation of men as sinners as its logical prius.

The fault of the division of opinion now in question is that it seeks to lift the question of the discrimination on God's part between men, by which they are divided into two classes, the one the recipients of his undeserved favor, and the other the objects of his just displeasure, out of the region of reality; and thus loses itself in mere abstractions. When we bring it back to earth we find that the question which is raised amounts to this: whether God discriminates between men in order that he may save some; or whether he saves some in order that he may discriminate between men. Is the proximate motive that moves him an abstract desire for discrimination, a wish that he may have some variety in his dealings with men; and he therefore determines to make some of the objects of his ineffable favor and to deal with others in strict accordance with their personal deserts, in order that he may thus exercise all his faculties? Or is it the proximate motive that moves him an unwillingness that all mankind should perish in their sins; and, therefore, in order to gratify the promptings of his compassion, he intervenes to rescue from their ruin and misery an innumerable multitude which no man can number—as many as under the pressure of his sense of right he can obtain the consent of his whole nature to relieve from the just penalties of their sin—by an expedient in which his justice and mercy meet and kiss each other? Whatever we may say of the former question, it surely is the latter which is oriented aright with respect to the tremendous realities of human existence.

One of the leading motives in the framing of the supralapsarian scheme, is the desire to preserve the particularistic principle throughout the whole of God's dealings with men; not with respect to man's salvation only, but throughout the entire course of the divine action with respect to men. God from creation itself, it is therefore said, deals with men conceived as divided into two classes, the recipients respectively of his undeserved favor and of his well-merited reprobation. Accordingly, some supralapsarians place the decree of discrimination first in the order of thought, precedent even to the decree of creation. All of them place it in the order of thought precedent to the decree of the fall. It is in place therefore to point out that this attempt to particularize the whole dealing of God with men is not really carried out, and indeed cannot in the nature of the case be carried out. The decree to create man, and more particularly the decree to permit the man whose creation is contemplated to fall into sin, are of necessity universalistic. Not some men only are created, nor some men created differently from others; but all mankind is created in its first head, and all mankind alike. Not some men only are permitted to fall; but all men and all men alike. The attempt to push particularism out of the sphere of the plan of salvation, where the issue is diverse (because confessedly only some men are saved), into the sphere of creation or of the fall, where the issue is common (for all men are created and all men are fallen), fails of the very necessity of the case. Particularism can come into question only where the diverse issues call for the postulation of diverse dealings looking toward the differing issues. It cannot then be pushed into the region of the divine dealings with man prior to man's need of salvation and God's dealings with him with reference to a salvation which is not common to all. Supralapsarianism errs therefore as seriously on the one side as universalism does on the other. Infralapsarianism offers the only scheme which is either self-consistent or consistent with the facts.

It will scarcely have escaped notice that the several conceptions of the nature of the plan of salvation which we have passed in review do not stand simply side by side as varying conceptions of that plan, each making its appeal in opposition to all the rest. They are related to one another rather as a progressive series of corrections of a primal error, attaining ever more and more consistency in the embodiment of the one fundamental idea of salvation. If, then, we wish to find our way among them it must not be by pitting them indiscriminately against one another, but by following them regularly up the series. Supernaturalism must first be validated as against Naturalism, then Evangelicalism as against Sacerdotalism, then Particularism as against Universalism; and thus we shall arrive at length at the conception of the plan of salvation which does full justice to its specific character. It is to this survey that attention will be addressed in the succeeding lectures.

The accompanying diagram will exhibit in a synoptical view the several conceptions which have been enumerated in this lecture, and may facilitate the apprehension of their mutual relations.

THE ORDER OF DECREES

Supralapsarian	Infralapsarian	Amyraldian	Lutheran	Wesleyan	Pure Universalistic	Anglican	Roman	Orthodox Greek	Remonstrant	Pelagian
Election of some to eternal life with God.	Permission of Fall — guilt, corruption and total inability.	Permission of Fall — corruption, guilt and moral inability.	Permission of Fall — guilt, corruption and total inability.	Permission of Fall — guilt, corruption and total inability.	Permission of Fall.	Permission of sin.	Permission of Fall — loss of supernatural righteousness.	Permission of Fall — loss of original righteousness, involving loss of knowledge of God and proneness to evil.	Permission of Fall — (physical) deterioration (followed by moral).	Gift of free will by virtue of which each may do all that is required of him.
Permission of Fall — guilt, corruption and total inability.	Election of some to life in Christ.	Gift of Christ to render salvation possible to all.	Gift of Christ to render satisfaction for the sins of the world.	Gift of Christ to render satisfaction for the sins of the world.	Predestination of all to life.	Gift of Christ to make satisfaction for the sins of all men.	Gift of Christ to offer satisfaction for all human sins.	Gift of Christ to reconcile sinful mankind with God.	Gift of Christ to render gift of sufficient grace possible.	Gift of the law and gospel to illuminate the way and persuade to walk in it.
Gift of Christ to redeem the elect and ground offer to all.	Gift of Christ to redeem his elect and ground offer to all.	Election of some for gift of moral ability.	Gift of means of grace to communicate saving grace.	Remission of original sin to all and gift to all of sufficient grace.	Gift of Christ to expiate the sin of all.	Establishment of Church as living agent for communicating God's sufficient grace.	Institution of the Church and the sacraments, to apply satisfaction of Christ.	Establishment of the Church "for the continual supply of the benefits of the cross."	Gift of sufficient (suasive) grace to all.	Gift of Christ to (expiate past sin and to) set good example.
Gift of the Holy Spirit to save the redeemed.	Gift of the Holy Spirit to save the redeemed.	Gift of the Holy Spirit to work moral ability in the elect.	Predestination to life for those who do not resist the means of grace.	Predestination to life of those who improve sufficient grace.	Gift of the Spirit to apply the expiation of Christ to all.	Communication of this grace through the sacraments as indispensable channels.	Application of satisfaction of Christ through sacraments, under operation of second causes.	Instruction, justification and edification through the ordinances of the Church.	Salvation of all who freely co-operate with this grace.	Acceptance of all who walk in right way.
Sanctification of all the redeemed and regenerated.	Sanctification of all the redeemed and regenerated.	Sanctification by the Spirit.	Sanctification through the means of grace.	Sanctification of all who cooperate with sufficient grace.	Salvation of all.	Salvation through the sacrament of baptism imparting life and of the Eucharist nourishing it.	Building up in holy life of all to whom the sacraments are continued.	Building up in grace through the seven sacraments.	Sanctification by co-operation with grace.	Continuance in right-doing by voluntary effort.

Column groupings (header hierarchy):

- **Supernaturalistic** (Supralapsarian – Orthodox Greek) | **Naturalistic** (Remonstrant, Pelagian)
  - **Evangelical** (Supralapsarian – Pure Universalistic) | **Sacerdotal** (Anglican, Roman, Orthodox Greek)
    - **Particularistic** (Supralapsarian – Amyraldian) | **Universalistic** (Lutheran, Wesleyan, Pure Universalistic)
      - **Consistently Particularistic** (Supralapsarian, Infralapsarian) | **Inconsistently Particularistic** (Amyraldian)

Lecture 2

Autosoterism

It is not of him that willeth,
nor of him that runneth,
but of God that hath mercy.

—Romans 9:16

Autosoterism

THERE ARE fundamentally only two doctrines of salvation[1]: that salvation is from God, and that salvation is from ourselves. The former is the doctrine of common Christianity; the latter is the doctrine of universal heathenism. "The principle of heathenism," remarks Dr. Herman Bavinck,[2] "is, negatively, the denial of the true God, and of the gift of his grace; and, positively, the notion that salvation can be secured by man's own power and wisdom. 'Come, let us build us a city, and a tower, whose top may reach unto heaven, and let us make us a name.' Gen. 11:4. Whether the works through which heathenism seeks the way of salvation bear a more ritual or a more ethical characteristic, whether they are of a more positive or of a more negative nature, in any case man remains his own saviour; all religions except the Christian are autosoteric. . . . And philosophy has made no advance upon this: even Kant and Schopenhauer, who, with their eye on the inborn sinfulness of man recognize the necessity of a regeneration, come in the end to an appeal to the will, the wisdom and the power of man."

It was quite apposite, therefore, when Jerome pronounced Pelagianism, the first organized system of self-salvation taught in the Church, the "heresy of Pythagoras and Zeno."[3] It was

in effect the crystallization in Christian forms of the widely
diffused Stoic ethics, by which the thought of men had been
governed through the whole preceding history of the Church.[4]
Around the central principle of the plenary ability of the human
will, held with complete confidence and proclaimed, not in the
weak negative form that obligation is limited by ability, but in
the exultant positive form that ability is fully competent to all
obligation, Pelagius, no mean systematizer, built up a complete
autosoteric system.[5] On the one side this system was protected
by the denial of any "fall" suffered by mankind in its first
head, and accordingly of any entail of evil, whether of sin or
mere weakness, derived from its past history. Every man is
born in the same condition in which Adam was created; and
every man continues throughout life in the same condition in
which he is born. By his fall Adam at most has set us a bad
example, which, however, we need not follow unless we
choose; and our past sins, while of course we may be called to
account for them and must endure righteous punishment on
their account, cannot in any way abridge or contract our
inherent power of doing what is right. "I say," declares
Pelagius, "that man is able to be without sin, and that he is
able to keep the commandments of God."[6] And this ability
remains intact after not only Adam's sin but any and every sin
of our own. It is, says Julian of Eclanum, "just as complete
after sins as it was before sins."[7] At any moment he chooses,
therefore, any man can cease all sinning and from that instant
onward be and continue perfect. On the other hand, this round
assertion of entire ability to fulfill every righteousness is
protected by the denial of all "grace," in the sense of inward
help from God. As such help from God is not needed, neither
is it given; every man in the most absolute sense works out his
own salvation: whether with fear and trembling or not, will
depend solely on his particular temperament. To be sure the

term "grace" is too deeply imbedded in the Scriptural represen-
tations to be altogether discarded. The Pelagians therefore
continued to employ it, but they explained it after a fashion
which voided it of its Scriptural pregnancy. By "grace" they
meant the fundamental endowment of man with his inalienable
freedom of will, and along with that, the inducements which
God has brought to bear on him to use his freedom for good.

The Pelagian scheme therefore embraces the following
points. God has endowed man with an inalienable freedom of
will, by virtue of which he is fully able to do all that can be
required of him. To this great gift God has added the gifts of
the law and the gospel to illuminate the way of righteousness
and to persuade man to walk in it; and even the gift of Christ
to supply an expiation for past sins for all who will do
righteousness, and especially to set a good example. Those
who, under these inducements and in the power of their
ineradicable freedom, turn from their sins and do righteousness,
will be accepted by the righteous God and rewarded according
to their deeds.

This was the first purely autosoteric scheme published in
the Church, and it is thoroughly typical of all that has succeeded it from that day to this.

In the providence of God the publication of this autosoteric
scheme was met immediately by an equally clear and consistently worked-out assertion of the doctrine of "grace," so that
the great conflict between grace and free will was fought out
for the Church once for all in those opening years of the fifth
century. The champion of grace in this controversy was
Augustine, whose entire system revolved around the assertion
of grace as the sole source of all good in man as truly and as
completely as did that of Pelagius around the assertion of the
plenary ability of the unaided will to work all righteousness.
The reach of Augustine's assertion is fairly revealed by the

demands of the Council of Carthage of A. D. 417-418, which refused to be satisfied by anything less than an unequivocal acknowledgement that "we are aided by the grace of God, through Christ, not only to know but also to do what is right, in each single act, so that without grace we are unable to have, think, speak, or do anything pertaining to piety." The opposition between the two systems was thus absolute. In the one, everything was attributed to man; in the other, everything was ascribed to God. In them, two religions, the only two possible religions at bottom, met in mortal combat: the religion of faith and the religion of works; the religion which despairs of self and casts all its hope on God the Saviour, and the religion which puts complete trust in self; or since religion is in its very nature utter dependence on God, religion in the purity of its conception and a mere quasi-religious moralism. The battle was sharp, but the issue was happily not doubtful. In the triumph of Augustinianism it was once for all settled that Christianity was to remain a religion, and a religion for sinful men, needing salvation, and not rot down into a mere ethical system, fitted only for the righteous who need no salvation.

But, as we have been told that the price of liberty is eternal vigilance, so the Church soon found that religion itself can be retained only at the cost of perpetual struggle. Pelagianism died hard; or rather it did not die at all, but only retired more or less out of sight and bided its time; meanwhile vexing the Church with modified forms of itself, modified just enough to escape the letter of the Church's condemnation. Into the place of Pelagianism there stepped at once Semi-pelagianism; and when the controversy with Semi-pelagianism had been fought and won, into the place of Semi-pelagianism there stepped that semi-semi-pelagianism which the Council of Orange betrayed the Church into, the genius of an Aquinas systematized for her, and the Council of Trent finally fastened with rivets of iron upon that portion of the church which obeyed it. The necessity of grace had been acknowledged as the result of the Pelagian controversy: its preveniency, as the result of the Semi-pelagian controversy: but its certain efficacy, its "irresistibility" men call it, was by the fatal compromise of Orange denied, and thus the conquering march of Augustinianism was checked and the pure confession of salvation by grace alone made forever impossible within that section of the Church whose proud boast is that it is *semper eadem*. It was no longer legally possible, indeed, within the limits of the Church to ascribe to man, with the Pelagian, the whole of salvation; nor even, with the Semi-pelagian, the initiation of salvation. But neither was it any longer legally possible to ascribe salvation so entirely to the grace of God that it could complete itself without the aid of the discredited human will—its aid only as empowered and moved by prevenient grace indeed, but not effectually moved, so that it could not hold back and defeat the operations of saving grace.

The gravitation of this Synergistic system is obviously downward, and therefore we cannot be surprised to learn that it easily fell away into that express Semi-pelagianism which, despite its official condemnation by the Church, seems to have formed the practical faith of most men throughout the Middle Ages, and in which the determining act in salvation is assigned, not to the grace of God conveying salvation, but to the consent of the will, giving to the almighty grace of God its efficacy. Here is a work-salvation as truly though not as grossly as in pure Pelagianism itself; and accordingly, throughout the Middle Ages, Legalism reigned supreme, a legalism which wrought precisely the same effects as are so vividly described by Heinrich Weinel, as manifesting themselves in the Jewish circles from which the Apostle Paul sprung. "He only can be happy under a dispensation of law," says Weinel,[8] "who can live a life-long lie. . . . But proud, downright, consistent natures cannot be put off with a lie. If they are unable to resist, they die of the lie; if they are strong, it is the lie that dies. The lie inherent in the law was the presumption that it could be fulfilled. Every one of Paul's associates understood that the commandment could not be kept, but they did not own it to themselves. The elder behaved in presence of the younger as if it could be kept; one believed it on the strength of another, and did not acknowledge the impossibility to himself. They blinded themselves to their own sin by comparing themselves with other just men, and had recourse to remote ages to Enoch and Noah and Daniel, in order to produce advocates for their souls.[9] They hoped God would allow the good works of the saints to cover their deficiencies, and they did not forget occasionally to pray for mercy, yet, on the whole they kept up the lie and went on as if they were well."

This is a true picture of the Middle Ages. Men knew very well that they could not earn for themselves salvation even under the incitement of the grace of God; they knew very well that they failed in their "good works," at every stage; and yet they kept the ghastly fiction up.[10] Were there no strong men "to kill the lie"? Strong men rose here and there, a Gottschalk in the ninth century, a Bradwardine, a Wyclif in the fourteenth, a Huss in the fifteenth, a belated Jansen in the seventeenth; but, despite their protests, the lie still lived on until at last the really strong man came in Martin Luther, and the lie died. The Augustianianism that had been repressed in the Church of Rome could not be suppressed. The Church had bound itself in that it might not contain it. There was nothing for it then but that it should burst the bounds of the Church and flow out from it. The explosion came in what we call the Reformation. For the Reformation is nothing other than Augustianianism come to its rights: the turning away from all that is human to rest on God alone for salvation.

Accordingly, nothing is more fundamental in the doctrine of the Reformers than the complete inability of man and his absolute need of divine grace;[11] and against nothing do the Reformers set their faces more firmly than the ascription to man of native power to good. To Luther, Pelagianism was the heresy of heresies, from the religious point of view equivalent to unbelief, from the ethical point of view to mere egotism. It was "for him the comprehensive term for all that which he particularly wishes to assault in the Catholic Church."[12] His treatise *De Servo Arbitrio* written against Erasmus' Pelagianizing exaltation of human ability, was esteemed by him the only one of his books, except the Catechism, in which he could find nothing to correct.[13] "As to the doctrine of free will as preached before Luther and other Reformers appeared," writes Calvin,[13a] "What effect could it have but to fill men with an overweening opinion of their own virtue, swelling them out with vanity, and leaving no room for the grace and assistance of the Holy Spirit." "When we tell a man," he writes again,[14] "to seek righteousness and life outside of himself, that is in Christ only, because he has nothing in himself but sin and death, a controversy immediately arises with reference to the freedom and power of the will. For if man has any ability of his own to serve God, he does not obtain salvation entirely by the grace of Christ, but in part bestows it on himself. Though we deny not that man acts spontaneously and of free will when he is guided by the Holy Spirit, we maintain that his whole nature is so imbued with depravity that of himself, he possesses no ability to act aright."[15]

It was not long, however, before, even in these circles of realized Augustinianism, in which the ascription of salvation to God alone was something like a passion, the old leaven of

self-salvation began to work again.[16] It was in no less a person
than Philip Melanchthon that this new "falling from grace"
entered into the thought of the Reformation, though in his
teaching it made but little progress. Three periods are distinguishable in the development of his doctrine.[17] In the first of
these he was as pure an Augustinian as Luther or Calvin
himself. In the second, commencing in 1527, he begins to go
to school to Aristotle in his general doctrine of the will. In
the third, from 1532 on, he allows the will of man, though
only as a purely formal power, some place in the very process
of salvation: it can put the spiritual affections created solely by
the Holy Spirit in chains or on the throne. From this beginning, synergism rapidly took form in the Lutheran Church.[18]
It met with opposition, it is true: the old Lutherans, an
Amsdorf, a Flacius, a Wigand, a Brenz were all fully convinced
Augustinians. But the opposition was not as hearty as it might
have been had the controversy with the Calvinists not been at
its height. Even Brenz permitted Strigel to taunt him at the
Weimar Disputation with his predestinationism, without boldly
taking the offensive. And so Andrea could corrupt Luther's
doctrine at the Conference at Mompelgard, 1586, without
rebuke;[19] Aegidius Hunnius could teach openly the resistibility
of grace;[20] and John Gerhard could condition election on the
foresight of faith.[21]   When Melanchthon toyed with such
ambiguous phrases as "God draws the willing to him," "Free
will is man's power to apply himself to grace," he was playing
with fire. A hundred years later the Saxon theologians, Hoe
van Hohenegg and Polycarp Leyser at the Leipzig Conference
of March 1631 could confidently present as Lutheran doctrine
the declaration that "God certainly chose us out of grace in
Christ; but this took place according to his foresight of who
would truly and constantly believe in Christ; and whom God
foresaw that they would believe, those he predestined and

elected to make blessed and glorious." The wonder-working grace of God which raises the dead that Luther so passionately proclaimed, was now put wholly at the disposal of that will of man which Luther declared to be utterly enslaved to sin and capable of moving in good part only as it is carried along and borne forward by grace.[22]

Nor have things bettered with the passage of the years. It is one of the best esteemed Lutheran teachers of our own day Wilhelm Schmidt, Professor of Theology at Breslau, who tells us[23] that "the divine purpose and love is able to realize itself only with and very precisely through the will of the being to whom it is directed;" and "in one word there exists over against God's holy decrees a freedom established by himself, against which they are often enough shattered, and may indeed in every individual case be shattered."[24] Accordingly he is not content to reject the *praedestinatio stricte dicta* of the Calvinists, but equally repudiates the *praedestinatio late dicta* of the old Lutheran divines, that teaches a decree of God by which all men are designated to salvation by an antecedent will, while by a consequent will all those are set apart and ordained to salvation, who, God foresees, "will finally believe in Christ." For, says he,[25] "with the divine, that is to say, the infallible foresight of them, the decisions of man cease to be free." Thus not only is the divine predestination but also the divine foresight sacrificed on the altar of human freedom, and the conclusion of the whole matter is enunciated in the words: "All men are, so far as concerns God, written in the Book of Life (*benevolentia universalis*); but who of them all stays written in it, is finally determined only at the end of the day." The result cannot be known beforehand, even by God.[26] It is not enough that redemption should engage the will, so that we may say that there is no redemption "except the sinner very energetically cooperate with it," even if this be interpreted to mean, "permits himself to be redeemed."[27]   We must go on and say that "redemption must fail of its end and remain without effect, however much the divine will of love and counsel of salvation might wish otherwise, if effect is not given it by man's inwardly bringing it to pass that, out of his own initiative, he grasps the rescuing hand and does repentance, breaks with his sin and leads a righteous life."[28]   When Schmidt comes, therefore to speak of the Application of Salvation by the Holy Spirit,[29] he is explicit in denying to the Holy Spirit any power to produce salvation in an unwilling soul.   "Even the Holy Spirit," he tells us, "can in the presence of the free will that belongs to man as such by nature, compel no one to accept salvation.   Even he can accomplish his saving purpose with us only if we do not obstruct, do not withdraw from, do not oppose his work for us.   All this stands in our power and he is helpless (*ohnmachtig*) with respect to it if we misuse it. . . . He who wills not to be saved cannot be helped even by the Holy Spirit."[30]

Self-assertion could scarcely go further; not even in those perhaps stirring but certainly somewhat blustering verses by W. E. Henley:

> Out of the night that covers me,
>   Black as the pit from pole to pole,
> I thank whatever Gods may be
>   For my unconquerable soul.
>
> In the fell clutch of circumstance
>   I have not winced nor cried aloud,
> Under the bludgeonings of chance
>   My head is bloody, but unbowed.
>
> Beyond this place of wrath and tears
>   Looms but the Horror of the shade,

And yet the menace of the years
Finds and shall find me unafraid.

It matters not how strait the gate,
　How charged with punishment the scroll,
I am the master of my fate:
　I am the captain of my soul.

This is of course Pelagianism unashamed—unless we should prefer to call it sheer heathenism. And yet it is cited with warm approval by an esteemed minister of the Church of Scotland, writing in quite its spirit on the great subject of "Election." He uses it indeed immediately to support a cheerful assertion of the fundamental Pelagian principle that ability limits obligation: "That conscious life which speaks saying, 'Thou oughtest,' wakes a no less certain echo within, which says, 'Because I ought I can.' That 'can' abides forever, however enfeebled it may become."[31] Pelagius could ask nothing more.

It may be inferred from such a phenomenon as that which has been mentioned that the Reformed Churches, though retaining their Augustinian confession as the Lutheran could not, and sloughing off the Arminian Semi-pelagianism which rose in the early seventeenth century to vex them as the Lutherans could not their synergism, have yet in our own day become honeycombed with the same Pelagianizing conceptions. This is so far true that we are met on all hands to-day, even in the Reformed Churches, with the most unmeasured assertions of human independence, and of the uncontrollableness and indeed absolute unpredictableness of the action of the human will. The extremes to which this can go are fairly illustrated by certain, no doubt somewhat incidental, remarks made by Dr. David W. Forrest in the unhappy book which he calls, certainly very misleadingly, "The Authority of Christ" (1906). In his hands human freedom has grown so all-powerful as fairly to abolish not only the common principles of evangelical religion but all faith in divine providence itself. He has adopted in effect a view of free agency which reserves to man complete independence and excludes all divine control or even foresight of human action. Unable to govern the acts of free agents, God is reduced to the necessity of constantly adjusting himself to them. Accordingly God has to accept in his universe much that he would much prefer should not be there. There is, for example, the whole sphere of the accidental. If we cooperate with others in dangerous employments, or, say, go out seeking pleasure with a shooting party, we may be killed by an unskillful act of a fellow workman or by the random shot of a careless marksman. God is helpless in the matter, and there will be no use in appealing to him with regard to it. For, says Dr. Forrest,[32] "God could only prevent the bad workman or marksman from causing death to others by depriving him of his freedom to shape his own course." There is in a word no providential control whatever of the acts of free agents. Accordingly, Dr. Forrest tells us,[33] a wise man will not be surprised that tragic cruelties should occur in the world, which seem almost un-alleviatedly wrong: "he will recognize the possibilities of man's freedom in defying God's will, both by the infliction of suffering and by the refusal to be taught by suffering." Nor can God's grace intervene to cure the defects of his providence. Human free will interposes an effectual barrier to the working of his grace; and God has no power to overcome the opposition of the human heart. "There is no barrier to the entrance of the Holy Spirit into the heart," remarks Dr. Forrest with the air of making a great confession,[34] "except that created by the refusal of the heart to welcome him," obviously only another way of saying that the heart's refusal is an insuperable barrier to the entrance of the Holy

Spirit into it.[35] Accordingly, the progress of his kingdom in the world could not be forecast in its details by our Lord, but lay in his mind only as outlined in its general features. "He saw," says Dr. Forrest, "that 'conversion' had its human factor as well as its divine; and that the mighty works of God might be rendered impossible by man's perversities of unbelief. Hence the detailed course of the kingdom in the world was an inscrutable thing. . . ."[36] Even in the Church itself the divine purpose may fail, despite the presence in the Church of the Spirit of God promised to it: for, though the Spirit will not fail to guide the Church, the Church may fail to "fulfill the conditions under which it could avail itself of the Spirit's guidance."[37] So zealous, in a word, is Dr. Forrest to emancipate man from the dominion of God that he goes near to placing God under the dominion of man. The world God has created has escaped beyond its tether; there is nothing for God to do but to accept it as he finds it and adjust himself as best he may to it. It was told to Thomas Carlyle once that Margaret Fuller had announced in her solemn way, "I accept the universe," "Gad, she'd better," was the simple comment of the sage. Is the Lord God Almighty in the same case?

If this be in any degree the case with God, why, of course there can be no talk of God's saving man. If man is to be saved at all, though it is questionable whether "saving" is the right word to use here, it is clear that he must "save" himself. If we can still speak of a plan of salvation on God's part, that plan must be reduced just to keeping the way of salvation open, that man, who is the master of his own destiny,[38] may meet with no hindrance when he chooses to walk in it. In very truth, this is the conception of "salvation" which in the widest circles is now confidently proclaimed. This is the hinge, indeed, on which turns the entire thought of that New Protestantism which has arisen in our day, repudiating the Reformation and all its works as mere medievalism, and attaching itself rather to the Enlightenment, as the birth of a new world, a new world in which rules just Man, the Lord of all. "Rationalism" we have been accustomed to call the whole movement, and as phase of it follows phase of it, in the Rationalismus Vulgaris of Wegscheider, we will say; in Kant and his followers; in the post-Kantian Schools; and now in our "New Protestantism" we must at least accord it the praise of breeding marvelously true to type.

Profound thinkers like Kant and perhaps we may say, even more, spiritually minded thinkers like Rudolf Eucken, may be incapable of the shallow estimate of human nature which sees in it nothing but good. But even the perception of the radical evil of human nature cannot deliver them out of the fixed circle of thought which asserts human ability for the whole sphere of human obligation, however that ability be construed. "How it is possible for a naturally bad man to make himself a good man," exclaims Kant,[39] "entirely baffles our thought, for how can a corrupt tree bring forth good fruit?" But he is, despite the perceived impossibility of it, able to rest in the solution, or rather no solution, of the weak, "It must be possible for us to become better, even if that which we are able to do should be of itself insufficient, and all that we could do was to make ourselves receptive for a higher assistance of an inscrutable kind."[40] Beyond a similar appeal to an inscrutable mystical power flowing through the life of the man who strives to help himself, even a Rudolf Eucken does not get. And so our most modern thought only reproduces the ancient Pelagianism, with a less profound sense of the guilt and a little deeper sense of the difficulties which evil has brought upon man. Of expiation it will hear nothing; and while it makes a place for aid, it must be an aid which flows into the soul in response to and along the lines of its own creative efforts.

Outside the deeper philosophies even this falls away, and the shallowest forms of Pelagianism stalk abroad with utter freedom from all sense of insufficiency. The most characteristic expression of this general point of view is given, perhaps, in the current adduction of the parable of the Prodigal Son as embodying not merely the essence but the entirety of the gospel. Precious as this parable is for its great message that there is joy in heaven over one sinner that repents, when it is perverted from the purpose for which it was spoken and made to stand for the whole gospel (*corruptio optimi pessima*), it becomes the instrument for tearing down the entire fabric of Christianity. There is no atonement in this parable, and indeed no Christ in even the most attenuated function which could possibly be ascribed to a Christ. There is no creative grace in this parable; and indeed no Holy Spirit in any operation the most ineffective that could be attributed to him. There is no seeking love of God in this parable: the father in the parable pays absolutely no attention to his errant son, just lets him alone, and apparently feels no concern about him. Considered as a pictorial representation of the gospel, its teaching is just this, and nothing more: that when anyone, altogether of his own motion, chooses to get up and go back to God, he will be received with acclamation. It is certainly a very flattering gospel. It is flattering to be told that we can get up and go to God whenever we choose, and that nobody is going to pester us about it. It is flattering to be told that when we choose to go back to God we can command a handsome reception, and no questions asked. But is this the gospel of Jesus Christ? Is the whole teaching of Jesus Christ summed up in this: that the gates of heaven stand open and anybody can go in whenever he pleases? That is, however, what the entire body of modern Liberal theologians tell us: our Harnacks and Boussets and their innumerable disciples and imitators.

"Innumerable" disciples and imitators, I say: for surely this teaching has overspread the world. We are told by Erich Schader that during his professorial life no student has ever come before him on the mind of whom the presentation of the two parables of the Pharisee and the Publican praying in the temple and of the Lost Son, in the sense that the forgiveness of God is conditioned by nothing and no atonement is needed, has not made for a longer or shorter time a great and deep impression.[41] It is a Pelagianism, you see, which out-pelagianizes Pelagius. For Pelagius had some recognition of the guilt of sin, and gave some acknowledgement of the atoning work of Christ in making expiation for this guilt. And this theology does neither. With no real sense of guilt, and without the least feeling for the disabilities which come from sin, it complacently puts God's forgiveness at the disposal of whosoever will deign to take it from his hands. The view of God which is involved, some one has not inaptly if a little bitingly called "the domestic animal conception of God." As you keep sheep to give you wool, and cows to give you milk, so you keep God to give you forgiveness. What is meant is grimly illustrated by the story of poor Heinrich Heine, writhing on his bed of agony, who, asked by an officious visitor if he had hope of the forgiveness of his sins, replied with a glance upwards of mocking bitterness, "Why, yes, certainly: that's what God is for." That's what God is for! It is thus that our modern Liberal theology thinks of God. He has but one function and comes into contact with man at but one point: he exists to forgive sins.

In somewhat the same spirit we hear ringing up and down the land the passionate proclamation of what its adherents love to call a "whosoever will gospel." It is no doubt the universality of the gospel-offer which is intended to be emphasized. But do we not shoot beyond the mark when we seem to hang salvation purely on the human will? And should we not stop to consider that, if so we seem to open salvation to "*whosoever will*" on the one hand, on the other we open it only to "whosoever will"? And who, in this world of death and sin, I do not say merely will, but can, will the good? Is it not forever true that grapes are not gathered from thorns, nor figs from thistles; that it is only the good tree which brings forth good fruit while the evil tree brings forth always and everywhere only evil fruit? It is not only Hannah More's Black Giles the Poacher who may haply "find it difficult to repent when he will." It is useless to talk of salvation being for "whosoever will" in a world of universal "won't." Here is the real point of difficulty: how, where, can we obtain *the will*? Let others rejoice in a "whosoever will gospel": for the sinner who knows himself to be a sinner, and knows what it is to be a sinner, only a "God will" gospel will suffice. If the gospel is to be committed to the dead wills of sinful men, and there is nothing above and beyond, who then can be saved?

As a recent writer, who makes no great claims to special orthodoxy but has some philosophical insight points out, "the self that is to determine is the same as the self that is to be determined"; "the self which according to Pelagius is to make one good is the bad self that needs to be made good." "The disease is in the will, not in some part of ourselves other than the will which the will can control. How can the diseased will provide the cure?"[42] "The seat of the problem is our wills; we could be good if we would, but we won't; and we can't begin to will it, unless we will so to begin, that is, unless we already will it. 'Who shall deliver me from the body of this death? I thank my God through Jesus Christ our Lord.' I am told to repent if I would be forgiven; but how can I repent? I only do what is wrong because I like it, and I can't stop liking it or like something else better because I am told to do so, nor even because it is proved that it would be better for me. If I am to be changed, something must lay hold of me and change me."[43] "Can peach renew lost bloom?" asks Christina G. Rossetti, more poetically, but with the same pungent point:

> Can peach renew lost bloom,
> Or violet lost perfume,
> Or sullied snow turn white as over-night?
> Man cannot compass it, yet never fear;
> The leper Naaman
> Shows what God will and can.
> God who worked then is working here;
> Wherefore let shame, not gloom, betinge thy brow.
> God who worked then is working now.

It is only in the loving omnipotence and omnipotent love of God that a sinner can trust.   "Christ" cries Charles H. Spurgeon,[44] "is not 'mighty to save' those who repent, but is able to make men repent. He will carry those to heaven who believe; but he is moreover mighty to give men new hearts, and to work faith in them. He is mighty to make the man who hates holiness, love it, and to constrain the despiser of his name to bend the knee before him. Nay, this is not all the meaning, for the divine power is equally seen in the after-work. . . . He is mighty to keep his people holy after he has made them so, and to preserve them in fear and love, until he consummates their spiritual existence in heaven."

If it were not so, the case of the sinner were desperate. It is only in almighty grace that a sinner can hope; for it is only almighty grace that can raise the dead. What boots it to send the trumpeter crying amid the serried ranks of the dead: "The gates of heaven stand open: whosoever will may enter in"? The real question which presses is, Who will make these dry bones live? As over against all teaching that would tempt man to trust in himself for any, even the smallest part, of his salvation, Christianity casts him utterly on God. It is God and God alone who saves, and that in every element of the saving process. "If there be but one stitch," says Spurgeon aptly, "in the celestial garment of our righteousness which we ourselves are to put in, we are lost."

Lecture 3

Sacerdotalism

The Lord added to them
day by day those that were saved.

—Acts 2:47

Sacerdotalism

I<small>T</small> <small>IS</small> <small>THE</small> consistent testimony of the universal Church that
salvation is from God, and from God alone. The tendency
constantly showing itself in all branches of the Church alike
to conceive of salvation as, in one way or another, to a greater
or less degree, from man, is thus branded by the entire Church
in its official testimony as a heathen remainder not yet fully
eliminated from the thinking and feeling of those who profess
and call themselves Christians. The incessant reappearance of
this tendency in one or another form throughout the Church is
evidence enough, however, of the difficulty which men feel in
preserving in its purity the Christian ascription of salvation to
God alone. And this difficulty obtrudes itself in another way
in a great and far-reaching difference which has arisen in the
organized testimony of the Church itself with respect to the
mode of the divine operation in working salvation in men.

Though salvation is declared to be wholly of God, who
alone can save, it has yet been taught in a large portion of the
Church (up to today in the larger portion of the Church), that
God in working salvation does not operate upon the human
soul directly but indirectly; that is to say, through instrumentalities
which he has established as the means by which his saving

grace is communicated to men. As these instrumentalities are committed to human hands for their administration, a human factor is thus intruded between the saving grace of God and its effective operation in the souls of men; and this human factor indeed, is made the determining factor in salvation.[45] Against this Sacerdotal system, as it is appropriately called, the whole Protestant Church, in all its parts, Lutheran and Reformed, Calvinistic and Arminian, raises its passionate protest. In the interests of the pure supernaturalism of salvation it insists that God the Lord himself works by his grace immediately on the souls of men, and has not suspended any man's salvation upon the faithfulness or caprice of his fellows. In the words of old John Hooper, it condemns as "an ungodly opinion" the notion "that attributeth the salvation of man unto the receiving of an external sacrament," "as though God's Holy Spirit could not be carried by faith into the penitent and sorrowful conscience except it ride always in a chariot and external sacrament."[46] In opposition to this "ungodly opinion" Protestantism suspends the welfare of the soul directly, without any intermediaries at all, upon the grace of God alone.

The sacerdotal principle finds very complete expression in the thoroughly developed and logically compacted system of the Church of Rome. According to this system God the Lord does nothing looking to the salvation of men directly and immediately: all that he does for the salvation of men he does through the mediation of the Church, to which, having endowed it with powers adequate to the task, he has committed the whole work of salvation.[47] "It is hardly incorrect to say," remarks Dr. W. P. Paterson in expounding the doctrine of the Church of Rome on this point,[48] "that in the Roman Catholic conception the central feature of the Christian religion is the supernatural institution which represents Christ, which carries on his work, and which acts as the virtual mediator of the blessings of salvation. Its vocation or commission is nothing less than the perpetuation of the work of the Redeemer. It does not, of course, supersede the work of Christ. Its pre-supposition is that Christ, the Eternal Son of God, laid the foundation of its work in his incarnation and his atoning death; that from him come ultimately all power, authority and grace; and that as from him all spiritual blessing proceeds, so to him belongs all the glory. But in the present dispensation, the Church, in large measure, has taken over the work of Christ. It is in a real sense, a reincarnation of Christ to the end of the continuation and completion of his redemptive mission. Through his Church he continues to execute the offices of a Prophet, of a Priest, and of a King. His prophetic office it perpetuates by witnessing to the truth once delivered to the saints, and by interpreting and determining doctrine with an infallible authority that carries the same weight and assurance as his own original revelation. It succeeds him on earth in the exercise of the priestly office. It represents him so completely in the priestly function of mediation between God and man, that even as there is none other name given among men than that of Jesus, whereby we must be saved, so there is no covenanted salvation outside the visible organization of which he is the unseen Head. It is further conceived that it represents him as sacrificing priest by the perpetual repetition in the Mass of the oblation which he once offered on the cross. In this divine sacrifice which is celebrated in the Mass, it is taught,[49] 'that same Christ is contained and immolated in an unbloody manner on the altar of the cross; and this sacrifice is truly propitiatory.' And, finally, it administers the kingly power of Christ on earth. It has an absolute claim to the obedience of its members in all matters of faith and duty, with the right and duty to punish the disobedient for the breach of its laws, and to coerce the contumacious."

In one word, the Church in this system is conceived to be Jesus Christ himself in his earthly form, and it is therefore substituted for him as the proximate object of the faith of Christians.[50] "The visible Church," says Mohler,[51] "is the Son of God, as he continuously appears, ever repeats himself, and eternally renews his youth among men in human form. It is his perennial incarnation." It is to the Church, then, that men must look for their salvation; it is from the Church and its ordinances alone that salvation is communicated to men; in a word it is to the Church rather than to Christ or to the grace of God that the salvation of men is immediately ascribed. Only "through the most holy sacraments of the Church," it is declared plainly,[52] is it, "that all true justice either begins; or being begun is increased; or being lost, is repaired." "The radical religious defect of the conception," comments Dr. Paterson justly,[53] "is that it makes the sinner fall into the hand of man, rather than into the hand of the all-merciful God. We look to God for salvation, and we are referred to an institution, which in spite of its lofty claims, is too manifestly leavened and controlled by the thoughts of men like ourselves." And again:[54] "The radical error of the Roman system was that the visible Church, which is human as much as it is divine, and which has become increasingly human, had largely thrust itself in the place of God and of the Saviour: and to the deeper religious insight it appeared that men were being invited and required to make the unsatisfactory venture of entrusting themselves to provisions and laws of human origin as the condition of attaining to the divine salvation. It was felt that the need of the soul was to press past the insecure earthly instrument, with its mediatorial claims and services, to the promises of God and to a finished work of the divine Saviour, and to look to God for the better assurance of truth and salvation which is given inwardly by the Holy Spirit of God.

The Protestant revision, in short, was more than justified by the religious need of basing salvation on a purely divine foundation, and of dispensing with ecclesiastical machinery which was largely human in its origin and conception." The question which is raised in sacerdotalism, in a word, is just whether it is God the Lord who saves us, or it is men, acting in the name and clothed with the powers of God, to whom we are to look for salvation. This is the issue which divides sacerdotalism and evangelical religion.

The essence of the sacerdotal scheme as it regards the actual salvation of individual men, may perhaps be fairly expressed by saying that, according to it, God truly desires (or, as the cant phrase puts it, wills by an antecedent conditional will) the salvation of all men, and has made adequate provision for their salvation in the Church with its sacramental system: but he commits the actual work of the Church and its sacramental system to the operation of the second causes through which the application of grace through the Church and its sacramental system is effected. As this system of second causes has not been instituted with a view to the conveying of the sacraments to particular men or to the withholding of them from particular men, but belongs to his general provision for the government of the world, the actual distribution of the grace of God through the Church and the sacraments lies outside the government of his gracious will. Those who are saved by obtaining the sacraments, and those who are lost by missing the sacraments, are saved or are lost therefore, not by the divine appointment, but by the natural working of second causes. God's antecedent conditional will that all should be saved, that is, on the condition of their receiving grace through the sacraments distributed under the government of second causes, is supplanted by a consequent absolute will of salvation, therefore, only in the case of those who, he foresees, will under the government of second causes, actually receive the sacraments and the grace which is conveyed by them. Thus, it is supposed, God is relieved from all responsibility with regard to the inequality of the distribution of saving grace. By his antecedent conditional will he wills the salvation of all. That all are not saved is due to the failure of some to receive the requisite grace through the sacraments. And their failure to receive the sacraments and the grace conveyed in them is due solely to the action of the second causes to which the distribution of the sacraments has been committed, that is, to the working of a general cause, quite independent of God's antecedent will of salvation. This seems to satisfy the minds of the sacerdotal reasoners. To the outsider it seems to mean only that God, having made certain general provisions for salvation, commits the salvation of men to the working of the general system of second causes; that is to say, he declines to be concerned personally about the salvation of men and leaves men to "nature" for the chances of their salvation.

The whole matter is very precisely expounded by an acute Jesuit writer, William Humphrey S. J.,[55] with particular reference to the special case of infants dying unbaptized (and, therefore, inevitably lost), which is looked upon apparently as a peculiarly hard case, requiring very careful treatment. It will repay us to follow his exposition.

"The order of thought," he tells us, "is as follows. Consequent on prevision of original sin, and the infection of the whole human race therewith, through the free transgression of Adam, its progenitor and head, God in his mercy wills the restoration of the whole human race. To this end he destines from eternity, and promises, and sends in the fulness of time, his Incarnate Son, with nature assumed from the same human race. He wills that this Incarnate Son, who is the Christ, should exhibit full satisfaction for all sins. This satisfaction, as foreseen, he accepts. At the appointed time, the Christ actually offers it for all human sins. 'God sent his Son that the world should be saved by him.' 'He is the propitiation for the sins of the whole world.' In the restored human race all are comprehended, even those who die in infancy, before use of reason. In the will of redemption all these infants, therefore, are comprehended. In the divine will that accepts the satisfaction, and in the human will of Christ which offers satisfaction, for all human sins, there is also an acceptance and offering of satisfaction for the original sin wherewith all these infants are infected. Hence, in view and in virtue of the merits and blood-shedding of Christ, God institutes for all these infants a sacrament, by means of which there might be applied to every one of them the merits and satisfaction of Christ. All these provisions have, by their nature, been ordained by God for the salvation of infants.

"A will of salvation which is such as this is, is no mere complacence in the goodness of the object regarded by itself; and, in this case, complacence in the goodness of salvation. It is on the part of God, an active and operative will of the salvation of infants. To all and every one of them this will of redemption is related.

"God wills to effect application of the sacrament of baptism, not by himself immediately, but by means of second causes; and through these second causes not to all infants by absolute will, but to all infants in so far as second causes, disposed in accordance with his universal and ordinary providence, do act under it.

"Among these second causes are, in the first place, the free wills of human beings, on which application of the sacrament, in the case at least of very many infants, is dependent. These human wills God anticipates, excites and inclines by his precepts, counsels, and aids, both of the natural order and of the supernatural order.   He thus provides that through the diligence and solicitude of those concerned; through their obedience and cooperation with grace received; through congruous merits and good works; through the alms-deeds and the prayers especially of the parents, and of those to whose guardianship the little ones have been confided, and through the apostolic labors of his ministers, the infants should be brought to the grace of baptism. As in the natural order, so also in the supernatural order of sanctification and eternal salvation, God wills to provide for infants through other human beings, and in accordance with the demands of the general laws of divine providence.

"In this way the divine will of salvation acts on the wills of men to procure the salvation of at least many infants who, nevertheless, by fault of men are not saved.   With regard to these infants, the antecedent will of God is an active will, that they should be saved; although it is not absolute, but under condition, that men on their part should second the divine will, as they can and ought to do, and although, consequently on contrary action on the part of men, God permits death in original sin, and, on prevision of this, does not will with a consequent will the salvation of those infants.

"Besides the wills of the human beings, which are in the moral order, and are free; there are also second causes of the physical order, and these are not free.   These causes contribute, in accordance with the common and ordinary laws of providence, to render bestowal of baptism either possible or impossible. The course of these causes, and the universal laws by which they are governed, God, consequently to original sin, wills to remain such as they now are.   God has not restored the preternatural state of immortality, even after the redemption of the human race by Christ had been decreed and effected. Hence, in accordance with the ordinary course of these laws, there follows the death of many infants before use of reason; and this sometimes independently of all exercise of will, and free action, of human beings.

"With this natural course of events, there is thoroughly consistent an antecedent conditional will in God of the salvation of all these infants. The condition under which he wills the application to them of baptism is—so far as the general order, which has been justly and wisely instituted, permits.

"If God had willed this order of physical causes of itself to the end that infants should die in original sin he certainly could not be said to will the salvation of these infants. God has not however instituted that order to this end nor does he so direct it by his will. He wills it for other ends, and those most wise ends.

"Hence, God does not directly intend the consequent death of infants in sin. He only permits it, in as much as he does not will to hinder, for all infants, the natural demands of physical laws, by a change of the general order, or through continual miracles.

"Such a permission proves only, that there is not in God an absolute will of the salvation of these infants. It in no way proves that there is not in God a conditional will of the salvation of all of them.

"In short, God wills the salvation of all infants who die in original sin by an antecedent will, in accordance with his common providence. In his common providence God predefines for everything a certain end, he conceives and prepares sufficient means in order to the obtaining of that end, he leaves everything to use these means, in accordance with the demand of its nature. That is to say, he leaves natural and necessary causes to act naturally and necessarily, contingent causes to act contingently, and free causes to act freely."

But enough!   The whole scheme is now certainly before us; and the whole scheme (generalizing from the particular instance treated) obviously is just this: that God has made sufficient provision for the salvation of all men, placed this provision in the world under the government of the ordinary course of nature, and left the actual salvation of men to work itself out in accordance with this ordinary course of nature. It is a kind of Deistic conception of the plan of salvation: God introduces into the concourse of causes by which the world is governed a new set of causes, working confluently in with them, making for salvation, and then leaves to the interworking of these two sets of causes the grinding out of the actual results.   He will not "change the general order"; and he will not inwork in the general order by "continuous miracles."   He just commits salvation to the general order as actually established.   This obviously is at best to attribute the salvation of the individual to God, only in the sense in which you attribute to God every other event which befalls him; it takes place under the operation of general laws.   There is no special supernaturalism in his salvation, though he be saved by the operation of specially supernatural instrumentalities inserted into the order of the world.   God retires behind his works, and man, if he be saved at all, is saved by law.

If we ask therefore why, on this scheme, one man is saved rather than another, we must answer, Because the sacraments come to one and not to the other.   If we ask why the sacraments come to one rather than to another, we must answer, Because the general order of providence, wisely and justly instituted for the government of the world, permits them to come to the one and not to the other; and the free agents involved, under the command of God, freely concur to that end in the one case and not in the other.   If we ask whether it is not God who has so disposed providence as to produce these precise effects, we must answer, No, for the general order of providence was instituted for the general wise government of the world and these particular effects are merely incidental to it. If we press on and ask, Could not God have so arranged his general providence as to have produced better results, and could he not so govern the world as to secure all else he wished and yet the salvation of men in greater numbers and with more particularity of choice on his part, we are dumb. For there is a manifest subjection of God's activities here to the working of the instrumentalities which he has ordained; there is a manifest subordination of God in his operations to second causes; or, to put it in another way, there is a manifest removal of man in the matter of his salvation from the direct control of God and the commitment of him instead to the tender mercies of a mechanism.

The explanation of Christianity in terms of sacerdotalism is unfortunately not confined in our day to the old unreformed Church from which Protestantism broke forth, precisely that it might escape from dependence on the Church rather than on God alone in the matter of salvation. A very influential, (perhaps presently the most influential, and certainly to the onlooker, the most conspicuous) party in the great Protestant Church of England, and, following it, large parties in its daughter Churches, have revived it in more or less completeness of expression and certainly with no hesitancy of assertion. It is common nowadays to hear men referred by Anglican writers to the Church rather than directly to God for salvation; and to have the Church defined for them as the "extension of the incarnation."[56] "To anyone who thinks carefully, and believes in the Incarnation," we are told by an influential clergyman of the Church of England,[57] with all the accent of conviction, "it is evident that the Church, the Body of Christ, ever united with her divine Head, holds in herself the forces

of his life," and therefore is "equipped," not merely to speak
for its Lord, but prevalently "to apply to the individual soul
the grace won for his Church by our blessed Redeemer, and
residing in that Body because ever united to the Head." The
whole sacerdotal system is wrapped up in that statement. The
Church, Mr. Darwell Stone tells us,[58] is a visible society, the
work of which is twofold, corresponding to the work of the
Lord, as expressed in John 1:17: "Grace and truth came by
Jesus Christ": "the Church, as his mystical body and his organ
in the world, is the teacher of truth and the storehouse of
grace." "Since the day of Pentecost the day of creation of the
Christian Church," he further explains,[59] "the ordinary way in
which God bestows grace on the souls of men is through the
glorified humanity of our Lord, and the work of God the Holy
Ghost. The closest means of union with the glorified humanity
of Christ, and the most immediate mode of contact with God
the Holy Ghost, are in the mystical body of Christ, that is the
Church, and are open to men in the use of the sacraments.
Thus the Christian Church is the channel of grace." From this
beginning Mr. Stone goes on to expound the sacerdotal system
in a manner indistinguishable from its ordinary exposition in
the Church of Rome.

We will ask, however, an American divine to explain to us
the sacerdotal system as it has come to be taught in the
Protestant Episcopal Churches.[60] "Man," we read in Dr. A. G.
Mortimer's "Catholic Faith and Practice," "having fallen before
God's loving purpose could be fulfilled, he must be redeemed,
bought back from his bondage, delivered from his sin, reunited
once more to God, so that the Divine Life might flow again in
his weakened nature" (p. 65). "By his life and death Christ
made satisfaction for the sins of all men, that is, sufficient for
all mankind, for through the Atonement sufficient grace is
given to every soul for its salvation; but grace, though suffi-

cient, if neglected, becomes of no avail" (p. 82).[61] "The Incarnation and the Atonement affected humanity as a race only[62]. Some means, therefore, was needed to transmit the priceless gifts which flowed from them to the individuals of which the race was comprised, not only at the time when our Lord was on earth, but to the end of the world. For this need, therefore, our Lord founded the Church" (p. 84). "Thus the Church became the living agent by which the graces and blessings, which flowed from Christ were dispensed to each individual soul which would appropriate them" (p. 84). "The Church claims not only to be the teacher of the truth and the guide in morals, but . . . the dispenser of that grace which enables us to fulfil her laws" (p. 100), "the dispenser of that grace which alone can enable man to believe what is true, to do what is right, and to attain his true end, to serve God acceptably here, and to live with God happily hereafter" (p. 114). "The chief means of grace are the Sacraments" (p. 120). "They are the channels by which the spiritual gift is conveyed to our souls. . . . The Christian Sacraments, therefore, do not merely signify grace; they actually confer it. Hence they are called 'effectual' signs of grace. Their action is *ex opere operato*" (p. 122). "Baptism is absolutely necessary to salvation, for a person can have no life who has not been born. This is called the *'necessitas medii,'* since Baptism is the means by which the supernatural life is given to the soul and the individual is incorporated into Christ." "Without the help of (the Eucharist), salvation would be so difficult to attain as to be practically impossible" (p. 127). Here obviously is as express a sacerdotalism as that of the Church of Rome itself, from which, indeed, it has been simply borrowed. The Church has completely taken the place of the Spirit of God as the proximate source of grace, and the action of the divine Spirit in applying salvation is postponed to and made subject to the operations of the Church through its ordinances. Thus the soul is removed from immediate dependence on God and taught rather to come to the Church and to expect all endowments of grace directly from it.

A modified and much milder form of sacerdotalism is inherent in Confessional Lutheranism, and is continually rising to more or less prominence in certain phases of Lutheran thought, thus creating a high church party in the Lutheran Church also.   It has been the boast of Lutheranism that it represents, in distinction from Calvinism, a "conservative reformation."[63]   The boast is justified, as on other grounds, so also on this, that it has incorporated into its confessional system the essence of the sacerdotalism which characterized the teaching of the old Church.   Confessional Lutheranism, like Romanism, teaches that the grace of salvation is conveyed to men in the means of grace, otherwise not.   But it makes certain modifications in the sacerdotal teaching which it took over from the old Church, and these modifications are of such a far-reaching character as to transform the whole system.   We do not commonly hear in Lutheran sacerdotalism much of "the Church," which is the very *cor cordis* of Roman sacerdotalism: what we hear of instead is "the means of grace."   Among these "means of grace" the main stress is not laid upon the sacra-ments, but on "the Word," which is defined as the chief "means of grace."   And the means of grace are not represented as acting *ex opere operato* but it is constantly declared that they are effective only to faith.   I do not say the scheme is a consistent one: in point of fact it is honeycombed with inconsistencies.   But it remains sufficiently sacerdotal to confine the activities of saving grace to the means of grace, that is to say, to the Word and sacraments, and thus to interpose the means of grace between the sinner and his God.   The central evil of sacerdotalism is therefore present in this scheme in its full manifestation, and wherever it is fully operative we find men exalting the means of grace and more or less forgetting the true agent of all gracious operations, the Holy Spirit himself, in their absorption with the instrumentalities through which alone he is supposed to work. It is in a truly religious interest, therefore, that the Reformed, as over against the Lutherans, insist with energy that, important as are the means of grace, and honored as they must be by us because honored by God the Holy Spirit as the instruments by and through which he works grace in the hearts of men, yet after all the grace which he works by and through them he works himself not out of them but immediately out of himself, *extrinsecus accedens*.

There are three aspects of the working of the sacerdotal system which must be kept clearly in view, if we wish to appraise with any accuracy the injury to the religious interests which it inevitably works. These have been more or less expressly alluded to already, but it seems desirable to call particular attention to them formally and together.

In the first place, the sacerdotal system separates the soul from direct contact with and immediate dependence upon God the Holy Spirit as the source of all its gracious activities. It interposes between the soul and the source of all grace a body of instrumentalities, on which it tempts it to depend; and it thus betrays the soul into a mechanical conception of salvation. The Church, the means of grace, take the place of God the Holy Spirit in the thought of the Christian, and he thus loses all the joy and power which come from conscious direct communion with God. It makes every difference to the religious life, and every difference to the comfort and assurance of the religious hope, whether we are consciously dependent upon instrumentalities of grace, or upon God the Lord himself, experienced as personally present to our souls, working salvation in his loving grace. The two types of piety, fostered by dependence on instrumentalities of grace and by conscious communion with God the Holy Spirit as a personal Saviour, are utterly different, and the difference from the point of view of vital religion is not favorable to sacerdotalism. It is the interests of vital religion, therefore, that the Protestant spirit repudiates sacerdotalism. And it is this repudiation which constitutes the very essence of evangelicalism. Precisely what evangelical religion means is immediate dependence of the soul on God and on God alone for salvation.

In the second place, sacerdotalism deals with God the Holy Spirit, the source of all grace, in utter neglect of his personality, as if he were a natural force, operating, not when and where and how he pleases, but uniformly and regularly wherever his activities are released. It speaks of the Church as the "institute of salvation," or even as "the storehouse of salvation" with apparently complete unconsciousness that thus it is speaking of salvation as something which may be accumulated or stored for use as it may be needed. The conception is not essentially different from that of storing electricity, say, in a Leyden jar, whence it can be drawn upon for use. How dreadful the conception is may be intimated by simply speaking of it with frankness under its true forms of expression: it is equivalent to saying that saving grace, God the Holy Spirit, is kept on tap, and released at the Church's will to do the work required of it. It would probably be no exaggeration to say that no heresy could be more gross than that heresy which conceives the operations of God the Holy Spirit under the forms of the action of an impersonal, natural force. And yet it is quite obvious that at bottom this is the conception which underlies the sacerdotal system. The Church, the means of grace, contain in them the Holy Spirit as a salvation-working power which operates whenever and wherever it, we can scarcely say he, is applied.

And this obviously involves, in the third place, the subjection of the Holy Spirit in his gracious operations to the control of men. Instead of the Church and the sacraments, the means of grace, being conceived, as they are represented in the Scriptures, and as they must be thought of in all healthful religious conceptions of them, as instrumentalities which the Holy Spirit uses in working salvation, the Holy Spirit is made an instrument which the Church, the means of grace, use in working salvation. The initiative is placed in the Church, the means of grace, and the Holy Spirit is placed at their disposal. He goes where they convey him; he works when they release him for work; his operations wait on their permission; and apart from their direction and control he can work no salvation. It ought to be unnecessary to say that this is a degrading conception of the modes of activity of the Holy Spirit. Its affinities are not with religion in any worthy sense of that word, which implies personal relations with a personal God, but with magic. At bottom, it conceives of the divine operations as at the disposal of man, who uses God for his own ends; and utterly forgets that rather God must be conceived as using man for his ends.

It is to break away from all this and to turn to God the Holy Spirit in humble dependence upon him as our gracious Saviour, our personal Lord and our holy Governor and Leader, that evangelicalism refuses to have anything to do with sacerdotalism and turns from all the instrumentalities of salvation to put its sole trust in the personal Saviour of the soul.

Lecture 4

Universalism

Who loved me,
and gave himself up for me.

—Galatians 2:20

Universalism

THE EVANGELICAL note is formally sounded by the entirety of organized Protestantism. That is to say, all the great Protestant bodies, in their formal official confessions, agree in confessing the utter dependence of sinful man upon the grace of God alone for salvation, and in conceiving this dependence as immediate and direct upon the Holy Spirit, acting as a person and operating directly on the heart of the sinner. It is this evangelical note which determines the peculiarity of the piety of the Protestant Churches. The characteristic feature of this piety is a profound consciousness of intimate personal communion with God the Saviour, on whom the soul rests with immediate love and trust. Obviously this piety is individualistic to the core, and depends for its support on an intense conviction that God the Lord deals with each sinful soul directly and for itself. Nevertheless, in odd contradiction to this individualistic sentiment which informs all truly evangelical piety, there exists in Protestantism a widespread tendency to construe the activities of God looking to salvation not individualistically but universally, to assert, in one word, that all that God does looking toward the salvation of sinful man, he does not to or for individual men but to or for all men alike, making no distinctions. This is the characteristic contention of what we know as Evangelical Arminianism and of Evangelical Lutheranism and is the earnest conviction of large bodies of Protestants gathered in many communions, under many names.

On the face of it, it would seem that if it is God the Lord and he alone who works salvation, by an operation of his grace immediately upon the heart, (which is the core of the evangelical confession); and if all that God does looking to the salvation of men he does to and for all men alike, (which is the substance of the universalistic contention); why, then, all men without exception must be saved. This conclusion, it would seem, can be escaped only by relaxing in one way or another the stringency of one or the other of the assumed premises. It must either be held that it is not God and God alone who works salvation, but that the actual enjoyment of salvation hangs at a decisive point upon something in man, or something done by man (and then we have fallen out of our evangelicalism into the mere naturalism of autosoterism); or it must be held that God's gracious activities looking to salvation are not after all absolutely universal in their operation (and then we have fallen away from our asserted universalism); or else it would seem inevitable that we should allow that all men are saved. Consistent evangelicalism and consistent universalism can coexist only if we are prepared to assert the salvation by God's almighty grace of all men without exception.

Accordingly, there has always existed a tendency in those evangelical circles which draw back more or less decisively from ascribing a thoroughgoing particularism to God in the distribution of his grace, to assume the actual salvation of all men, provided, that is, that their sense of the complete dependence of the sinner upon God for salvation is strong and operative. Among the condemnations of errors included in the Summa Confessionis et Conclusionum of the Synod held at

Debreczen on February 24, 1567, we find a clause directed against what are there called the "Holopraedestinarii," which runs as follows:[64] "The Holy Scripture refutes by these reasons also the Holopraedestinarii, that is, those who imagine that the whole world is elected and that a universal predestination follows from the universal promise; and teaches that predestination is of a few, and is particular, and that the number of the elect is certain, and their catalogue extends to their very hairs. 'For the very hairs of your head are all numbered.' . . . But it does not at all follow from this doctrine that God is partial or a respecter of persons." Who these sixteenth century Holopraedestinarii were we have not been careful to inquire;[64a] but certainly, from that time to this, there have never lacked those who in the interest of protecting God from the charge of "partiality or respect of persons" have been inclined to hold that he has chosen all men to salvation and through his almighty grace brings them all to that blessed goal.

The most recent and perhaps the most instructive instances of this tendency are provided by two divines of the Church of Scotland of our own day, Dr. William Hastie, late Professor of Divinity in the University of Glasgow and Dr. William P. Paterson, now holding the Chair of Divinity, the Chair of Chalmers and Flint, in the University of Edinburgh. In his admirable Croall lectures on "The Theology of the Reformed Churches in its Fundamental Principles," Dr. Hastie announces that "the word of the eternal hope seems to me the latest message of the Reformed Theology;"[65] and Dr. Paterson takes up the hint and enlarges on it in the excellent chapter on "The Testimony of the Reformed Churches" included in his Baird Lecture on "The Rule of Faith."[66] Dr. Paterson considers that Calvinism contains in itself elements "which are mutually repulsive," in its "doctrine of everlasting punishment" on the one hand, and its "doctrine of election and irresistible grace" on the other.   Relief might no doubt be had, "when thought rebels against making God responsible" for the everlasting punishment of some "by a doctrine of reprobation," by taking refuge in "an Arminian or semi-Arminian type of thought." This relief would be purchased, however, at the too dear cost of abandonment of concinnity of thought, and of falling away from faithfulness to the evangelical principle, which is the core of Christianity.   There remains, then, according to Dr. Paterson, no other way but to discard the doctrine of everlasting punishment, and to "resolve reprobation into a temporary lack of privilege and of spiritual attainment."   And he somewhat complacently remarks that "it is a curious circumstance that, while Calvinism has become unpopular chiefly because of its identification with a grim and remorseless doctrine of eternal punishment, it is the only system which contains principles—in its doctrines of election and irresistible grace—that could make credible a theory of universal restoration."

What Dr. Paterson says in these last words is true enough: but it is true only because, when rightly considered, Calvinism, with its doctrines of election and irresistible grace, is the only system which can make credible the salvation of any sinner: since in these doctrines alone are embodied in its purity the evangelical principles that salvation is from God alone and from him only in the immediate working of his grace. Whether this grace in God's unspeakable mercy is granted to some men only or is poured out on all men alike, is a different question to be determined on its own grounds.   And this question is certainly not to be facilely resolved by the simple assumption that God's mercy must be poured out on all alike, since otherwise not all men can be saved.   The fundamental presupposition of such an assumption is no other than that God owes all men salvation, that is to say, that sin is not really sin and is to be envisaged rather as misfortune than as ill-desert.

That it is this low view of sin which is really determinative of the whole direction of Dr. Paterson's thought at this point becomes immediately apparent upon attending to the terms of his argument. "It has been customary to say," he reasons, "that as there would have been no injustice in the punishment of all guilty beings, there can be none in the punishment of some guilty beings out of the number. Those who are saved are saved because of the mercy of God, while those who are lost perish because of their sins. This is as true as to say that those sick persons who are saved by the skill and devotion of a physician owe their lives to him, and that those that die perish of their diseases; but in that case the physician does not escape censure if it can be shown that it was in his power to have treated and saved those who died. It is therefore impossible to say that the doctrine of the divine love is not affected, since on Calvinistic principle it is in the power of God to deal with all in the same way in which he has dealt with the rest. For *ex hypothesi* it is in the power of God, in virtue of the principle of irresistible grace, to save even the worst, and if nevertheless there is a part of the human race which is consigned to everlasting punishment, it seems to be only explicable on the assumption that the divine love is not perfect, because it is not an all-embracing and untiring love."

Is it, then, inconceivable that the divine hand might be held back form saving all by something other than lack of power? The whole matter of the ill-desert of sin and the justice of God responding in hot indignation to this ill-desert, is left out of Dr. Paterson's reasoning. If the case were really as he represents it and men in their mere misery, appealing solely to God's pity, lay before the divine mind, it would be inexplicable that he did not save all. The physician who, having the power to treat and cure all his patients, arbitrarily discriminates between them and contents himself with ministering to some of them only, would justly incur the reprobation of men.   But may not the judge, having the mere power to release all his criminals, be held back by higher considerations from releasing them all?   It may be inexplicable why a physician in the case supposed should not relieve all; while the wonder may be in the case of the judge rather how he can release any.   The love of God is in its exercise necessarily under the control of his righteousness; and to plead that his love has suffered an eclipse because he does not do all that he has the bare power to do, is in effect to deny to him a moral nature.   The real solution to the puzzle that is raised with respect to the distribution of the divine grace is, then, not to be sought along the lines either of the denial of the omnipotence of God's grace with the Arminians, or of the denial of the reality of his reprobation with our neo-universalists, but in the affirmation of his righteousness.   The old answer is after all the only sufficient one: God in his love saves as many of the guilty race of man as he can get the consent of his whole nature to save.   Being God and all that God is, he will not permit even his ineffable love to betray him into any action which is not right.   And it is therefore that we praise him and trust him and love him.   For he is not part God, a God here and there, with some but not all the attributes which belong to true God: he is God altogether, God through and through, all that God is and all that God ought to be.

Meanwhile, it is not the consistent universalism that demands the actual salvation of all sinners, which has been embraced by the mass of universalizing Protestants.   For one thing, the Scriptures are too clear to the contrary to permit the indulgence of this pleasant dream: it is all too certain that all men are not saved, but at the last day there remain the two classes of the saved and the lost, each of which is sent to the eternal destiny which belongs to it.   The great problem requires to be faced by universalizing evangelicalism, therefore, of how it is God and God alone who saves the soul, and all that God does looking towards the saving of the soul he does to and for all men alike, and yet all men are not saved. Their attempts to solve this problem have given us the doctrinal constructions known as Evangelical Lutheranism and Evangelical Arminianism, both of which profess to combine an express evangelicalism and an express universalism, and yet to provide for the diverse issues of salvation and damnation. That these systems have succeeded in solving this (let us say it frankly, insoluble) problem, we of course do not believe; and the element in the problem which suffers in the forcible adjustments which they propose, is in both cases the evangelical element. But it is nevertheless to be frankly recognized that both systems profess to have found a solution and are therefore emphatic in their professions of both a pure evangelicalism and a complete universalism in the operation of God looking to salvation. It will be worth our while to make this clear to ourselves. In doing so, however, we shall choose statements from which we may learn something more of the spirit and points of view of these great systems than the particular facts which are more immediately engaging our attention.

How deeply embedded the evangelical conviction is in the consciousness of evangelical Arminianism we may learn from an instructive enunciation of it by Dr. Joseph Agar Beet.[67] This enunciation occurs in a context in which Dr. Beet is with some heat repelling the doctrine of unconditional election. "This terrible error," he says, "prevalent a century ago, is but an overstatement of the important Gospel truth that salvation is, from the earliest turning to God to final salvation, altogether a work of God in man, and a merciful accomplishment of a purpose of God before the foundation of the world." "In our rejection of this doctrine of unconditional election and predestination, we must remember that salvation, from the earliest good desires to final salvation, is the accomplishment of a divine purpose of mercy formed before the foundation of the world." In rejecting the doctrine of unconditional election, Dr. Beet is thus careful to preserve the evangelicalism which, he recognizes, lies at its center; and thus he gives us a definition of evangelicalism from the Wesleyan standpoint. It proves to be just that all the saving process is from God, and that all the power exerted in saving the soul is God's. It may please us in passing to ask whether this evangelicalism is really separable from the doctrine of unconditional election from which Dr. Beet wishes to separate it; and to note that he himself appears to recognize that in the minds of some at least the two must go together. But what it particularly behooves us to observe now is the emphasis with which, as a Wesleyan, Dr. Beet bears his testimony to the general evangelical postulate. Whether he gives validity to this postulate in all his thinking is of course a different matter.

From the Lutheran side the consciousness of the evangelical principle is equally prominent. Indeed the Evangelical Lutheran is very apt to look upon evangelicalism as his own peculiar possession, and to betray a certain measure of surprise when he finds it in the hands of others also. A. J. Haller, writing in Zahn and Burger's Magazine,[68] expresses himself in the following emphatic language: "That salvation is not acquired by man by means of any activity of his own, but is given him by God's grace, that I cannot believe in Jesus Christ my Lord or come to him of my own reason or power, but the Holy Spirit has called me, enlightened, sanctified and preserved me, this is assuredly the alpha and omega of all evangelical belief, and is not denied even by either Calvinists or Methodists." The purity of this evangelical confession must be frankly recognized, even though we cannot avoid cherishing misgivings whether it is permitted to condition all of the thought of its author, misgivings which are indeed immediately justified when we find him going on to speak of regeneration, and speaking of it after a fashion which is in spirit less evangelical than sacerdotal, and indeed is not untouched by the naturalism which usually accompanies this type of sacerdotalism. He is sure that regeneration is monergistic, but also that it is the effect of baptism as its producing cause; and he is very much concerned to defend this conception from the charge of magical working. "It might be called magical," he remarks,[69] "if it were maintained that men were completely transformed in regeneration, with no subsequent demand made upon them for any ethical self-determination. That, however, an absolutely new power is created in them by God, the saving or condemning action of which depends on their subsequent or contemporary determination (Entscheidung), this has as little to do with magic as the belief that in the Lord's Supper Christ's body and blood are certainly and truly given for blessing to some, for judgement to others."

A passage like this reveals the difficulty a Lutheran who wishes to abide by his official confession has in giving effect to his evangelical profession. He may declare that all the power exerted in saving the soul is from God, but this is crossed by his sacerdotal consciousness that grace is conveyed by the means of grace, otherwise not. The grace of regeneration, for example, is conveyed ordinarily (some say only) by baptism. And this grace of regeneration is the monergistic operation of God. Even so, however, it cannot be said that the effect is all of God. For, in the first place, whether it takes effect at all, is dependent on the attitude of the recipient. He cannot cooperate with God in producing it; but he can fatally resist. And therefore Baier[70] carefully defines: "God produces in the man who is baptized and who does not resist the divine grace, the work of regeneration or renovation through the Sacrament, in the very act itself (hoc actu ipso)." And then, in the second place, whether this gift of regeneration proves a blessing or a curse to the recipient depends on how he takes it and deals with it. "An absolutely new power is created in him by God," says Haller,[71] "the action of which, whether for blessing or cursing, is dependent on the subject's subsequent, or even already presently operative decision." This carries with it, naturally, what is here covered up, that this self-determination of the recipient is his natural self-determination. For if it were itself given in the new power communicated in regeneration, then it were inconceivable that it could act otherwise than for blessing. Whether man is saved or not, depends therefore in no sense on the monergistic regeneration wrought by God in his baptism. It depends on how man receives this "new power" communicated to him and how he uses it. And thus we are back on the plane of pure naturalism.

We may more than question therefore whether the cherished evangelicalism of the Wesleyan and Lutheran constructions is not more theoretical than practical;[71a] though meanwhile we must recognize that they at least postulate the evangelical principle in theory.

It is, however, the universalistic note which is the characteristic note of these constructions. As Professor Henry C. Sheldon of Boston University declares:[72] "Our contention is for the universality of the opportunity of salvation, as against an exclusive and unconditioned choice of individuals to eternal life." There is to be noted in this declaration, (1) the conscious stress on universalism as the characteristic note of Wesleyanism, and (2) the consequent recognition that all that God does looking toward salvation is to afford an opportunity of salvation; so that what is actually contended is not that God does not save some only but that he really saves none,—he only opens a way of salvation to all and if any are saved they must save themselves. So inevitable is it that if we assert that all that God does looking to salvation he does to and for all alike and yet that not all are saved, we make all that he does fall short of actual salvation: no one must receive more than he who receives the least.

Perhaps, however, the essential universalistic note of the whole Arminian construction never received a stronger assertion than in the creed of the Evangelical Union body, the so-called Morrisonians, the very reason of the existence of which is to raise protest against the unconditionality of election. Its positive creed in itself sums up in what it calls the "three universalities": "the love of God the Father in the gift and sacrifice of Jesus to all men everywhere without distinction, exception or respect of persons; the love of God the Son, in the gift and sacrifice of himself as a true propitiation for the sins of the world; the love of God the Holy Spirit, in his personal and continuous work of applying to the souls of all men the provisions of divine grace."[73] Certainly if God is to be declared to love all men alike, the Son to have made propitiation for the sins of all men alike, and the Holy Spirit to have applied the benefits of that propitiation to all men alike, nothing is left but to assert that therefore all men alike are saved; or else to assert that all that God can do for sinful man cannot avail to save him and he must just be left to save himself. And where then is our evangelicalism, with its great affirmation that it is God the Lord and he alone with his almighty grace who saves the soul?

A lurid light is thrown upon the real origin of these vigorous assertions of the universalism of God's saving activities by some remarks of a sympathetic historian in accounting for the rise of the Morrisonian sect.[74] "Of the movement now to engage our attention," he remarks, "nothing is truer than that it was the genuine offspring of its age. During the thirties of the last century the legislatures of our country were made to recognize the rights of man as they had never done before. In politics the long night of privilege was far spent, and the dawn of a new age was beginning to appear. Brotherhood, equality and fair play were clamoring loudly at every closed door, and refusing to be turned away. A corresponding claim, quite independent of politics, was being made in the name of Christian theology. Here also it has demanded that doors of privilege be thrown open. Freedom for all, food for all, education for all, and salvation for all were now coming to be the national watchwords." Words could scarce be chosen which could more sharply present the demand for "the three universalities" as the mere clamoring of the natural heart for the equal distribution of the goods of the other life as of this, as, in other words, but the religious aspect of the "leveling" demand which has filled our modern life. The cry, "Give us all an equal chance!" may have its relative justification when it is the expression of the need of men perishing under the heel of vested privilege. But what shall we say of it when it is but the turbulent self-assertion of a mob of criminals, assailing a court of justice, whence is dispensed not "chances" to escape just penalties, but wisely directed clemency, having in view all rights involved? Surely the evil desert of sin, the just government of God, and the unspeakable grace of salvation are all fatally out of mind when men reason as to the proper procedure of God in bringing sinners to salvation by the aid of analogies derived from the leveling politics of the day. Shall we not fix it once for all in our minds that salvation is the right of no man; that a "chance" to save himself is no "chance" of salvation for any; and that, if any of the sinful race of man is saved, it must be by a miracle of almighty grace, on which he has no claim, and, contemplating which as a fact, he can only be filled with wondering adoration of the marvels of the inexplicable love of God? To demand that all criminals shall be given a "chance" of escaping their penalties, and that all shall be given an "equal chance," is simply to mock at the very idea of justice, and no less, at the very idea of love.

The universalism of all the divine operations looking to salvation is as vigorously asserted in the Lutheran scheme as in the Arminian, but with, if possible, even less logical success—on the supposition, that is, that the evangelical principle of dependence on God alone for salvation is to be preserved. Indeed the leaven of sacerdotalism taken over by Lutheranism from the old church, in its doctrine of the means of grace, from the first fatally marred even the purity of its universalism, transmuting it into a mere indiscrimination, which is something very different; and has among the modern Lutherans given rise to very portentious developments.

The old Lutheranism, alleging that the honor of God required that he should do all that he does looking to the salvation of man to and for all men alike, asserted that therefore Christ has died to take away the sin of the whole world, and, provision having been made in the means of grace for the effective application of his sacrifice to all men, these means of grace (with the mind especially on the proclamation of the gospel in which they culminate), have actually been conveyed to all men without exception. Of course it is not in point of fact true that the gospel has been actually proclaimed to all men without exception; and an effort was accordingly made to cover up the manifest falsity of the assertion by substituting for it the essentially different proposition that at three historical stages (namely, at the time of Adam, at the time of Noah, and at the time of the apostles), the gospel has been made known to all men then living, "and," it is added, "if it became universal in those three generations then it has also come indirectly to their successors." The futility of this expedient to conceal the circumstance that in point of fact the gospel has not actually been conveyed to every single man who has ever lived (and nothing less than this can satisfy the demands of the case), is too manifest to require pointing out; and we cannot be surprised that the contention itself has ceased to be made. "More recent orthodox theologians in our church," the historian (the Norwegian divine, Lars Nielsen Dahle) goes on to tell us,[75] "say simply that the universality of the call is a necessary presupposition, a postulate which must be assumed on the ground of the testimony of Scripture regarding God's universal saving-will on the one hand, and of the Scripturally established truth on the other that this saving will cannot be realized for the individual unless God's call actually reaches him; but how this happens, we cannot say, for it is a fact that at the present day it has only reached comparatively few, or at most a minority of mankind." Thus Professor Johnson writes:[76] "The universality of this call of grace we must, in opposition to every particularistic view of it, maintain as a postulate of the faith, even if we are unable to show how it actually does reach every individual." It is an unsolved mystery.

The Lutherans, therefore, in attempting both to tie saving grace to the means of grace and to give it an actually universal diffusion, have brought themselves into a difficulty at this point from which the Wesleyans, who make the universality of the sacrificial work of Christ and the consequent gift of sufficient grace independent of all earthly transactions so that men are all born in a state of redemption and grace, are free. The ultimate solution which has been found by modern Lutheranism, in which Dahle himself concurs, consists in the invention of a doctrine of the extension of human probation into the next world, the famous doctrine miscalled that of a "second probation," for it is not a doctrine of a second probation for any man but only the doctrine that every man that lives must have the gospel presented winningly to him, if not in this life then in the life to come. By the invention of this doctrine the Lutherans have provided themselves for the first time with a true universalism of grace. There is confessionally no direct Biblical support for the doctrine: it is simply a postulate of the universalism of God's will of salvation in connection with the confinement of grace to the means of grace. The Scriptures teach that no man can be saved without a knowledge of Jesus Christ in his saving work. This is transmuted into its opposite that no man can be lost without a knowledge of Christ in his saving work; and then in the interests of this proposition provision is made for every man to be brought face to face with the offer of the gospel under favorable circumstances, if not in this world, then in the next. No doubt some such invention was necessary if the Lutheran premises were to be sustained. But one would think that the necessity for such an invention in order to sustain these premises were a sufficient indication that these premises were best abandoned.

Having by this invention avoided the fact that the provision for salvation is in point of fact not universal, the Lutherans have by no means escaped from their difficulties. They are faced with the even greater difficulty, common to them and the Wesleyans, of accounting for the failure of God's grace, now safely conveyed to all men, to work the salvation of all men. And here there is no outlet but that of the Wesleyans, namely to bring in surreptitiously the discredited naturalism, and to attribute the difference in the effects of grace to men's differences in dealing with grace. The Lutherans have their own way, however, of introducing this naturalism. They are emphatic that man, being dead in sin, cannot cooperate with the grace of God, a difficulty got over by Arminianism by the postulation of a graciously restored ability for all men, earned for them by the sacrifice of Christ and applied to them automatically. But they suppose that, though dead in sin, man can resist, and successfully resist, almighty grace. Resistance is, however, itself an activity: and the successful resistance of an almighty recreative power, is a pretty considerable activity—for a dead man. It all comes back, therefore, to the Pelagian ground that, at the decisive point, the salvation of man is in his own power: men are saved, or men are not saved, according to natural differences in men. Thus the grace of God is fundamentally denied and salvation is committed, in the last analysis, to man himself.

The upshot of the whole matter is that the attempt to construe the gracious operations of God looking to salvation universally, inevitably leads by one path or another to the wreck of the evangelical principle, on the basis of which all Protestant Churches, (or rather, let us say, of the supernaturalistic principle, on the basis of which all Christian Churches,) professedly unite. Whether this universalism takes a sacerdotal form or a form which frees itself from all entanglement with earthly transactions, it ends always and everywhere by transferring the really decisive factor in salvation from God to man. This is not always clearly perceived or frankly admitted. Sometimes, however, it is. Professor W. F. Steele of the University of Denver, for example, clearly perceives and frankly admits it. To him there can be no talk of "almighty grace." Occupying a position which is practically (whatever we may say of it theoretically) indistinguishable from the bumptious naturalism of Mr. W. E. Henley, the first article of his creed is a hearty belief in the almightiness of man in his sphere of moral choices. "When one says," he tells us,[77] "'I believe in God, the Father Almighty,' he means it with reserve for in the domain of man's moral choices under grace, man himself is almighty, according to God's self-limitation in making man in his image and after his likeness." God himself, he goes on to declare, has a creed which begins: "I believe in man, almighty in his choices." Obviously a man in this mood is incapable of religion, the very essence of which is the sense of absolute dependence on God, and is altogether inhibited from evangelicalism, which consists in humble resting on God and God alone for salvation. Instead of the real *Gloria soli Deo* ringing in his heart, he proudly himself seizes the helm and proclaims himself, apart from God, the master of his own destiny. Moralism has completely extruded religion. Did not Luther have precisely the like of this in mind when he satirically describes the moralist of his day in these striking words: "Here we are always wanting to turn the tables and do good of ourselves to that poor man, our Lord God, from whom we are rather to receive it"?[78]

The antipathy which is widely felt to the fundamental evangelical postulate which brings the soul into immediate contact with God and suspends all its health on the immediate operations of God, finds an odd illustration in Albrecht Ritschl's teaching that the direct object even of justification is not the individual but the Christian society; and that "it is passed on to the individual only as the result of his taking place in the Christian fellowship and sharing in its life."[79] This is, of course, only another, and very much poorer way of asserting the principle of the general universalistic construction: God does not in any stage of the saving process deal directly with individuals; he has always and everywhere the mass in view; and it is the part of the individual himself by his own act to lay hold of the salvation thus put at the general disposal. How different Luther with his: "it is not needful for thee to do this or that. Only give the Lord God the glory, take what he gives thee, and believe what he tells thee."[80] The issue is indeed a fundamental one and it is closely drawn. Is it God the Lord that saves us, or is it we ourselves? And does God the Lord save us, or does he merely open the way to salvation, and leave it according to our choice, to walk in it or not? The parting of the ways is the old parting of the ways between Christianity and autosoterism. Certainly only he can claim to be evangelical who with full consciousness rests entirely and directly on God and on God alone for his salvation.

Lecture 5

Calvinism

*As many as were ordained
to eternal life believed.*

—Acts 13:48

Calvinism

As over against all attempts to conceive the operations of God looking to salvation universalistically, that is as directed to mankind in the mass, Calvinism insists that the saving operations of God are directed in every case immediately to the individuals who are saved. Particularism in the processes of salvation becomes thus the mark of Calvinism. As supernaturalism is the mark of Christianity at large, and evangelicalism the mark of Protestantism, so particularism is the mark of Calvinism. The Calvinist is he who holds with full consciousness that God the Lord, in his saving operations, deals not generally with mankind at large, but particularly with the individuals who are actually saved. Thus, and thus only, he contends, can either the supernaturalism of salvation which is the mark of Christianity at large and which ascribes all salvation to God, or the immediacy of the operations of saving grace which is the mark of evangelicalism and which ascribes salvation to the direct working of God upon the soul, come to its rights and have justice accorded it. Particularism in the saving processes, he contends, is already given in the supernaturalism of salvation and in the immediacy of the operations of the divine grace; and the denial of particularism is constructively the denial of the immediacy of saving grace, that is, of evangelicalism, and of the supernaturalism of salvation, that is, of Christianity itself.   It is logically the total rejection of Christianity.

The particularism of the saving operations of God which is thus the mark of Calvinism, it is possible, however, to apply more or less fully (or, shall we say, with more or less discernment?) in our thought of the activities of God relatively to his sinful creatures (or shall we say, broadly, relatively to his creatures?). Thus differing varieties of Calvinism have emerged in the history of thought. As they are distinguishable from one another by the place they give to particularism in the operations of God, that is as much as to say they are distinguished from one another by the place they give to the decree of election in the order of the divine decrees.

Some are so zealous for particularism that they place discrimination at the root of all God's dealings with his creatures. That he has any creatures at all they suppose to be in the interest of discrimination, and all that he decrees concerning his creatures they suppose he decrees only that he may discriminate between them. They therefore place the decree of "election" by which men are made to differ, in the order of decrees, logically prior to the decree of creation itself, or at any rate prior to all that is decreed concerning man as man; that is to say, since man's history begins with the fall, prior to the decree of the fall itself. They are therefore called Supralapsarians, that is, those who place the decree of election in the order of thought prior to the decree of the fall.[81]

Others, recognizing that election has to do specifically with salvation, (that is to say, that it is the logical prius, not of creation or of the providential government of the world, but of the salvation of sinful man), conceive that the principle of particularism, in the sense of discrimination, belongs in the sphere of God's soteriological, not in that of his cosmical creation. They therefore think of "election" as the logical prius not of creation, or of the fall, but of those operations of God which concern salvation. The place they give it in the order of decrees is therefore at the head of those decrees of God which look to salvation. This implies that it falls into position in the order of thought, consequently upon the decrees of creation and the fall, which refer to all men alike, since all men certainly are created and certainly have fallen; and precedently to the decrees of redemption and its application, since just as certainly all men are not redeemed and brought into the enjoyment of salvation. They are from this circumstance called Sublapsarians or Infralapsarians, that is, those who, in the arrangement of the decrees in logical order, conceive the place of the decree of election to be logically after that of the fall.

There are others, however, who, affected by what they deem the Scriptural teaching concerning the universal reference of the redemption of Christ, and desirous of grounding the universal offer of salvation in an equally universal provision, conceive that they can safely postpone the introduction of the particularistic principle to a point within the saving operations of God themselves, so only they are careful to introduce it at a point sufficiently early to make it determinative of the actual issue of the saving work. They propose therefore to think of the provision of salvation in Christ as universal in its intent; but to represent it as given effect in its application to individuals by the Holy Spirit only particularistically. That is to say, they suppose that some, not all, of the divine operations looking to the salvation of men are universalistic in their reference, whereas salvation is not actually experienced unless not some but all of them are operative. As the particular saving operation to which they ascribe a universalistic reference is the redemption of Christ, their scheme is expressed by saying that it introduces the decree of election, in the order of thought, at a point subsequent to the decree of redemption in Christ. They may therefore be appropriately called Post-redemptionists, that is, those who conceive that the decree of election is logically postponed to the decree of redemption. In their view redemption has equal reference to all men, and it is only in the application of this redemption to men that God discriminates between men, and so acts, in this sense, particularistically.

It is obvious that this is the lowest point in the order of decrees at which the decree of election can be introduced and the particularistic principle be retained at all. If the application of the redemption of Christ by the Holy Spirit be also made universalistic, that is to say, if the introduction of the particularistic principle be postponed to the actual issue of the saving process, then there is obviously no particularism at all in the divine operations looking to salvation. "Election" drops out of the scheme of the divine decrees altogether, unless we prefer to say, as it has been cynically phrased, that God is careful to elect to salvation only those who, he foresees, will in the use of their own free will elect themselves. All Calvinists must therefore be either Supralapsarians or Sub- (or Infra-) lapsarians, or, at least, Post-redemptionists which is also to be Ante-applicationists.

Nevertheless, we do not reach in the Post-redemptionists, conceived purely from the point of view of this element of their thought, the lowest possible, or the lowest actual, variety of Calvinists. Post-redemptionists may differ among themselves, if not in the position in the order of decrees of the decree of election (for still further to depress its position in that order would be to desert the whole principle of particularism and to fall out of the category of Calvinists), yet in their mode of conceiving the nature of the work of the Holy Spirit in applying redemption, under the government of the decree of election; and as to the role of the human spirit in receiving redemption. A party has always existed even among Calvinists which has had so large an interest in the autonomy of the human will, that it has been unwilling to conceive of it as "passive" with respect to that operation of God which we call regeneration, and has earnestly wished to look upon the reception of salvation as in a true sense dependent on the will's own unmoved action. They have, therefore, invented a variety of Calvinism which supposes that it is God indeed who selects those who shall savingly be brought to Christ, and that it is the Holy Spirit who, by his grace, brings them infallibly to Christ, (thus preserving the principle of particularism in the application of salvation), but which imagines that the Holy Spirit thus effectually brings them to Christ, not by an almighty, creative action on their souls, by which they are made new creatures, functioning subsequently as such, but purely by suasive operations, adapted in his infallible wisdom to the precise state of mind and heart of those whom he has selected for salvation, and so securing from their own free action, a voluntary coming to Christ and embracing of him for salvation. There is no universalism here; the particularism is express. But an expedient has been found to enable it to be said that men come voluntarily to Christ, and are joined to him by a free act of their own unrenewed wills, while only those come whom God has selected so to persuade to come (he who knows the heart through and through) that they certainly will come in the exercise of their own free will. This type of thought has received the appropriate name of "Congruism," because the principle of its contention is that grace wins those to whom it is "congruously" offered, that is to say, that the reason why some men are saved and some are not lies in the simple fact that God the Holy Spirit operates in his gracious suasion on some in a fashion that is carefully and infallibly adapted by him to secure their adhesion to the gospel, and does not operate on others with the same careful adaptation.

A warning must, however, be added to the effect that the designation "Congruists" is so ambiguous that there exists another class bearing this name, who are as definitely anti-Calvinistic as those we have in mind are, by intention, Calvinistic in their conception. The teaching of these is that God the Holy Spirit accords his suasive influences to all alike, making no distinction; but that this universalistically conceived grace of the Holy Spirit takes effect only according as it proves to be actually congruous or incongruous to the state of mind and heart of those to whom it equally is given. Here it is not the sovereign choice of God, but a native difference in men, which determines salvation, and we are on expressly autosoteric ground. The danger of confusing the Calvinistic "Congruists" with this larger, and definitely anti-Calvinistic party, has led to the habit of speaking of the Calvinistic Congruists rather by the name of their most distinguished representative, (who, indeed, introduced this mode of thinking into the Calvinistic churches), Claude Pajon, Professor in the Theological School at Saumur in France in the middle of the seventeenth century. It was his predecessor and teacher in the same school, Moses Amyraut, who first formulated in the Reformed Churches the Post-redemptionist scheme, of which Pajonism is a debased form. Thus the school of Saumur has the bad eminence of having originated, and furnished from the names of its professors the current designations of, the two most reduced forms of Calvinism, Amyraldianism or Hypothetical Universalism as it is otherwise called, and Pajonism, or Congruism as it is designated according to its nature.

We have thus had brought before us four forms of Calvinism; and these, as we believe, exhaust the list of possible general types: Supralapsarianism, Sub- (or Infra-) lapsarianism, Post-redemptionism (otherwise called Amyraldianism, or Hypothetical Universalism), and Pajonism (otherwise called Congruism). These are all forms of Calvinism, because they give validity to the principle of particularism as ruling the divine dealings with man in the matter of salvation; and, as we have seen, the mark of Calvinism is particularism. If now, particularism were not only the mark of Calvinism but also the substance of Calvinism, all four of these types of Calvinism, preserving as they all do the principle of particularism, might claim to be not only alike Calvinistic, but equally Calvinistic, and might even demand to be arranged in the order of excellence according to the place accorded by each in its construction to the principle of particularism and the emphasis placed on it. Particularism, however, though the distinguishing mark of Calvinism, by which it may be identified as over against the other conceptions of the plan of salvation, in comparison with which we have brought it, does not constitute its substance; and indeed, although strenuously affirmed by Calvinism, is not affirmed by it altogether and solely for its own sake. The most consistent embodiment of the principle of particularism is not therefore necessarily the best form of Calvinism; and the bare affirmation of the principle of particularism though it may constitute one so far a Calvinist, does not necessarily constitute one a good Calvinist. No one can be a Calvinist who does not give validity to the principle of particularism in God's operations looking to the salvation of man; but the principle of particularism must not be permitted, as Pharaoh's lean kine devoured all the fat cattle of Egypt, to swallow up all else that is rich and succulent and good in Calvinism, nor can the bare affirmation of particularism be accepted as an adequate Calvinism.

Post-redemptionism, therefore (although it is a recognizable form of Calvinism, because it gives real validity to the principle of particularism), is not therefore necessarily a good form of Calvinism, an acceptable form of Calvinism, or even a tenable form of Calvinism. For one thing, it is a logically inconsistent form of Calvinism and therefore an unstable form of Calvinism. For another and far more important thing, it turns away from the substitutive atonement, which is as precious to the Calvinist as is his particularism, and for the safeguarding of which, indeed, much of his zeal for particularism is due. I say, Post-redemptionism is logically inconsistent Calvinism. For, how is it possible to contend that God gave his Son to die for all men, alike and equally; and at the same time to declare that when he gave his Son to die, he already fully intended that his death should not avail for all men alike and equally, but only for some which he would select (which, that is, because he is God and there is no subsequence of time in his decrees, he had already selected) to be its beneficiaries? But as much as God is God, who knows all things which he intends from the beginning and all at once, and intends all things which he intends from the beginning and all at once, it is impossible to contend that God intends the gift of his Son for all men alike and equally and at the same time intends that it shall not actually save all but only a select body which he himself provides for it. The schematization of the order of decrees presented by the Amyraldians, in a word, necessarily implies a chronological relation of precedence and subsequence among the decrees, the assumption of which abolishes God, and this can be escaped only by altering the nature of the atonement. And therefore the nature of the atonement is altered by them, and Christianity is wounded at its very heart.

The Amyraldians "point with pride" to the purity of their confession of the doctrine of election, and wish to focus attention upon it as constituting them good Calvinists. But the real hinge of their system turns on their altered doctrine of the atonement, and here they strike at the very heart of Calvinism. A conditional substitution being an absurdity, because the condition is no condition to God, if you grant him even so much as the poor attribute of foreknowledge, they necessarily turn away from a substitutive atonement altogether. Christ did not die in the sinner's stead, it seems, to bear his penalties and purchase for him eternal life; he died rather to make the salvation of sinners possible, to open the way of salvation to sinners, to remove all the obstacles in the way of salvation of sinners. But what obstacle stands in the way of the salvation of sinners, except just their sin? And if this obstacle (their sin) is removed, are they not saved? Some other obstacles must be invented, therefore, which Christ may be said to have removed (since he cannot be said to have removed the obstacle of sin) that some function may be left to him and some kind of effect be attributed to his sacrificial death. He did not remove the obstacle of sin, for then all those for whom he died must be saved, and he cannot be allowed to have saved anyone. He removed, then, let us say, all that prevented God from saving men, except sin; and so he prepared the way for God to step in and with safety to his moral government to save men. The atonement lays no foundation for this saving of men: it merely opens the way for God safely to save them on other grounds.

We are now fairly on the basis of the Governmental Theory of the Atonement; and this is in very truth the highest form of doctrine of atonement to which we can on these premises attain. In other words, all the substance of the atonement is evaporated, that it may be given a universal reference. And, indeed, we may at once recognize it as an unavoidable effect of universalizing the atonement that it is by that very act eviscerated. If it does nothing for any man that it does not do for all men why, then, it is obvious that it saves no man; for clearly not all men are saved. The things that we have to choose between, are an atonement of high value, or an atonement of wide extension. The two cannot go together. And this is the real objection of Calvinism to this compromise scheme which presents itself as an improvement on its system: it universalizes the atonement at the cost of its intrinsic value, and Calvinism demands a really substitutive atonement which actually saves. And as a really substitutive atonement which actually saves cannot be universal because obviously all men are not saved, in the interests of the integrity of the atonement it insists that particularism has entered into the saving process prior, in the order of thought, to the atonement.

As bad Calvinism as is Amyraldianism, Pajonism is, of course, just that much worse. Not content with destroying the whole substance of the atonement, by virtue of which it is precious ("Who loved *me*, and gave himself up for *me*"), it proceeds to destroy also the whole substance of that regeneration and renovation by which, in the creative work of the Spirit, we are made new creatures. Of what value is it that it should be confessed that it is God who determines who shall be saved, if the salvation that is wrought goes no deeper than what I can myself work, if I can only be persuaded to do it? Here there is lacking all provision not only for release from the guilt of sin, but also for relief from its corruption and power. There is no place left for any realizing sense of either guilt or corruption; there is no salvation offered from either the outraged wrath of a righteous God or the ingrained evil of our hearts: after all is over, we remain just what we were before. The prospect that is held out to us is nothing less than appalling; we are to remain to all eternity fundamentally just our old selves with only such amelioration of our manners as we can be persuaded to accomplish for ourselves. The whole substance of Christianity is evaporated, and we are invited to recognize the shallow remainder as genuine Calvinism, because, forsooth, it safeguards the sovereignty of God. Let it be understood once for all that the completest recognition of the sovereignty of God does not suffice to make a good Calvinist. Otherwise we should have to recognize every Mohammedan as a good Calvinist. There can be no Calvinism without a hearty confession of the sovereignty of God; but the acknowledgement of the sovereignty of God of itself goes only a very little way toward real Calvinism. Pajon himself, the author of Calvinistic Congruism, advanced in his fundamental thought but little beyond a high variety of Deism.

It seems particularly worth while to make these things explicit, because there is perhaps nothing which more prejudices Calvinism in the general mind than the current identification of it with an abstract doctrine of sovereignty, without regard to the concrete interests which this sovereignty safeguards. In point of fact the sovereignty of God for which Calvinism stands is not only the necessary implicate of that particularism without which a truly religious relation between the soul and its God cannot exist; but is equally the indispensable safeguard of that complementary universalism of redemption equally proclaimed in the Scripture in which the wideness of God's mercy comes to manifestation. It must be borne well in mind that particularism and parsimony in salvation are not equivalent conceptions; and it is a mere caricature of Calvinistic particularism to represent it as finding its center in the proclamation that there are few that are saved.[82] What particularism stands for in the Calvinistic system is the immediate dealing of God with the individual soul; what it sets itself against is the notion that in his saving processes God never comes directly into contact with the individual—is never to be contemplated as *his* God who saves *him*—but does all that he does looking to salvation only for and to men in the mass. Whether in dealing with the individual souls of men, he visits with his saving grace few or many, so many that in our imagination they may readily pass into all, does not lie in the question. So far as the principles of sovereignty and particularism are concerned, there is no reason why a Calvinist might not be a universalist in the most express meaning of that term, holding that each and every human soul shall be saved; and in point of fact some Calvinists (forgetful of Scripture here) have been universalists in this most express meaning of the term. The point of insistence in Calvinistic particularism is not that God saves out of the sinful mass of men only one here and there, a few brands snatched from the burning, but that God's method of saving men is to set upon them in his almighty grace, to purchase them to himself by the precious blood of his Son, to visit them in the inmost core of their being by the creative operations of his Spirit, and himself, the Lord God Almighty, to save them. How many, up to the whole human race in all its representatives, God has thus bought and will bring into eternal communion with himself by entering himself into personal communion with them, lies, I say, quite outside the question of particularism. Universalism in this sense of the term and particularism are so little inconsistent with one another that it is only the particularist who can logically be this kind of a universalist.

And something more needs to be said—Calvinism in point of fact has as important a mission in preserving the true universalism of the gospel (for there is a true universalism of the gospel) as it has in preserving the true particularism of grace. The same insistence upon the supernaturalistic and the evangelical principles, (that salvation is from God and from God alone, and that God saves the soul by dealing directly with it in his grace) which makes the Calvinist a particularist, makes him also a universalist in the scriptural sense of the word. In other words the sovereignty of God lays the sole foundation, for a living assurance of the salvation of the world. It is but a spurious universalism which the so-called universalistic systems offer: a universalism not of salvation but, at the most, of what is called the opportunity, the chance, of salvation. But what assurance can a universal opportunity, or a universal chance, of salvation (if we dare use such words) give you that all, that many, that any indeed, will be saved? This universal opportunity, chance, of salvation has, after two thousand years, been taken advantage of only by a pitiable minority of those to whom it has been supposed to be given. What reason is there to believe that, though the world should continue in existence for ten billions of billions of years, any greater approximation to a completely saved world will be reached than meets our eyes today, when Christianity, even in its nominal form, has conquered to itself, I do not say merely a moiety of the human race, but I say merely a moiety of those to whom it has been preached?[83] If you wish, as you lift your eyes to the far horizon of the future, to see looming on the edge of time the glory of a saved world, you can find warrant for so great a vision only in the high principles that it is God and God alone who saves men, that all their salvation is from him, and that in his own good time and way he will bring the world in its entirety to the feet of him whom he has not hesitated to present to our adoring love not merely as the Saviour of our own souls, but as the Saviour of the world; and of whom he has himself declared that he has made propitiation not for our sins only, but for the sins of the world. Calvinism thus is the guardian not only of the particularism which assures me that God the Lord is the Saviour of my soul, but equally of the universalism by which I am assured that he is also the true and actual Saviour of the world. On no other ground can any assurance be had either of the one or of the other. But on this ground we can be assured with an assurance which is without flaw, that not only shall there be saved the individual whom God visits with his saving grace, but also the world which he enters with his saving purpose, in all the length and breadth of it.

The redemption of Christ, if it is to be worthily viewed, must be looked at not merely individualistically, but also in its social, or better in its cosmical relations. Men are not discrete particles standing off from one another as mutually isolated units. They are members of an organism, the human race; and this race itself is an element in a greater organism which is significantly termed a universe. Of course the plan of salvation as it lies in the divine mind cannot be supposed to be concerned, therefore, alone with individuals as such: it of necessity has its relations with the greater unities into which these individuals enter as elements. We have only partially understood the redemption in Christ, therefore, when we have thought of it only in its modes of operation and effects on the individual. We must ask also how and what it works in the organism of the human race, and what its effects are in the greater organism of the universe. Jesus Christ came to save men, but he did not come to save men each as a whole in himself out of relation to all other men. In saving men, he came to save mankind; and therefore the Scriptures are insistent that he came to save the world, and ascribe to him accordingly the great title of the Saviour of the world. They go indeed further than this: they do not pause in expanding their outlook until they proclaim that it was the good pleasure of God "to sum up all things in Christ, the things in the heavens, and the things on the earth." We have not done justice to the Biblical doctrine of the plan of salvation therefore so long as we confine our attention to the modes of the divine operation in saving the individual, and insist accordingly on what we have called its particularism. There is a wider prospect on which we must feast our eyes if we are to view the whole land of salvation. It was because God loved the world, that he sent his only-begotten Son; it was for the sins of the world that Jesus Christ made propitiation; it was the world which he came to save; it is nothing less than the world that shall be saved by him.

What is chiefly of importance for us to bear in mind here, is that God's plan is to save, whether the individual or the world, by process. No doubt the whole salvation of the individual sinner enters into the full enjoyment of this accomplished salvation only by stages and in the course of time. Redeemed by Christ, regenerated by the Holy Spirit, justified through faith, received into the very household of God as his sons, led by the Spirit into the flowering and fruiting activities of the new life, our salvation is still only in process and not yet complete. We still are the prey of temptation; we still fall into sin; we still suffer sickness, sorrow, death itself. Our redeemed bodies can hope for nothing but to wear out in weakness and to break down in decay in the grave. Our redeemed souls only slowly enter into their heritage. Only when the last trump shall sound and we shall rise from our graves, and perfected souls and incorruptible bodies shall together enter into the glory prepared for God's children, is our salvation complete.

The redemption of the world is similarly a process. It, too, has its stages: it, too, advances only gradually to its completion. But it, too, will ultimately be complete; and then we shall see a wholly saved world. Of course it follows, that at any stage of the process, short of completeness, the world, as the individual, must present itself to observation as incompletely saved. We can no more object the incompleteness of the salvation of the world today to the completeness of the salvation of the world, than we can object the incompleteness of our personal salvation today (the remainders of sin in us, the weakness and death of our bodies) to the completeness of our personal salvation. Every thing in its own order: first the seed, then the blade, then the full corn in the ear. And as, when Christ comes, we shall each of us be like him, when we shall see him as he is, so also, when Christ comes, it will be to a fully saved world, and there shall be a new heaven and a new earth, in which dwells righteousness.

It does not concern us at the moment to enumerate the stages through which the world must pass to its complete redemption. We do not ask how long the process will be; we make no inquiry into the means by which its complete redemption shall be brought about. These are topics which belong to Eschatology and even the lightest allusion to them here would carry us beyond the scope of our present task. What concerns us now is only to make sure that the world will be completely saved; and that the accomplishment of this result through a long process, passing through many stages, with the involved incompleteness of the world's salvation through extended ages, introduces no difficulty to thought. This incompleteness of the world's salvation through numerous generations involves, of course, the loss of many souls in the course of the long process through which the world advances to its salvation. And therefore the Biblical doctrine of the salvation of the world is not "universalism" in the common sense of that term. It does not mean that all men without exception are saved. Many men are inevitably lost, throughout the whole course of the advance of the world to its complete salvation, just as the salvation of the individual by process means that much service is lost to Christ through all these lean years of incomplete salvation. But as in the one case, so in the other, the end is attained at last: there is a completely saved man and there is a completely saved world. This may possibly be expressed by saying that the Scriptures teach an eschatological universalism, not an each-and-every universalism. When the Scriptures say that Christ came to save the world, that he does save the world, and that the world shall be saved by him, they do not mean that there is no human being whom he did not come to save, whom he does not save, who is not saved by him. They mean that he came to save and does save the human race; and that the human race is being led by God into a racial salvation: that in the age-long development of the race of men, it will attain at last to a complete salvation, and our eyes will be greeted with the glorious spectacle of a saved world. Thus the human race attains the goal for which it was created, and sin does not snatch it out of God's hands: the primal purpose of God with it is fulfilled; and through Christ the race of man, though fallen into sin, is recovered to God and fulfills its original destiny.

Now, it cannot be imagined that the development of the race to this, its destined end, is a matter of chance; or is committed to the uncertainties of its own determination. Were that so, no salvation would or could lie before it as its assured goal. The goal to which the race is advancing is set by God: it is salvation. And every stage in the advance to this goal is, of course, determined by God. The progress of the race is, in other words, a God-determined progress, to a God-determined end. That being true, every detail in every moment of the life of the race is God-determined; and is a stage in its God-determined advance to its God-determined end. Christ has been made in very truth Head over all things for his Church: and all that befalls his Church, everything his Church is at every moment of its existence, every "fortune," as we absurdly call it, through which his Church passes, is appointed by him. The rate of the Church's progress to its goal of perfection, the nature of its progress, the particular individuals who are brought into it through every stage of its progress: all this is in his divine hands. The Lord adds to the Church daily such as are being saved. And it is through the divine government of these things, which is in short the leading onwards of the race to salvation, that the great goal is at last attained. To say this is, of course, already to say election and reprobation. There is no antinomy, therefore, in saying that Christ died for his people and that Christ died for the world. His people may be few today: the world will be his people tomorrow. But it must be punctually observed that unless it is Christ who, not opens the way of salvation to all, but actually saves his people, there is no ground to believe that there will ever be a saved world. The salvation of the world is absolutely dependent (as is the salvation of the individual soul) on its salvation being the sole work of the Lord Christ himself, in his irresistible might. It is only the Calvinist that has warrant to believe in the salvation whether of the individual or of the world. Both alike rest utterly on the sovereign grace of God.[84] All other ground, is shifting sand.

THE END

Notes

1. Cf. A. A. Hodge: "Outlines of Theology."[2] 1878, p. 96: "There are in fact, as we might have anticipated, but two complete self-consistent systems of Christian theology possible"—Augustinianism and Pelagianism.

2. *Geref. Dog.*[1] ii. pp. 425, 426.

3. Preface to Book IV of his work on Jeremiah. Cf. Milman, "Latin Christianity" i. p. 106, note 2; De Pressensée *Trois Prem. Siecles.* ii. p. 375; Hefele, "Councils," E. T. ii. p. 446, note 3; cf. Warfield, "Two Studies in the History of Doctrine," 1897, pp. 4, 5.

4. Not that the autosoteric idea ever really satisfied the religious heart. Cf. T. R. Glover, "Conflict of Religions, etc." p. 67: "That salvation was not from within was the testimony of every man who underwent the *taurobolium.* So far as such things can be, it is established by the witness of every religious mind that, whether the feeling is just or not, the feeling is invincible that the will is inadequate and that religion begins only where the Stoic idea of saving oneself by one's own resolve and effort is finally abandoned."

5. Similarly also Kant, *Religion innerhalb der Grenzen der blossen Vernunft (Gesammelte Schriften* 1907. Bd. VI): "If the moral law demands of us that we become better men, it follows unavoidably that it must be possible for us so to become."

6. "On Nature and Grace," 49.

7. "The Unfinished Work," i. 91.

8. "St. Paul," E. T. pp. 72, 73.

9. "That it was possible to keep the whole law is an idea that is frequent in the Talmud. Abraham, Moses, and Aaron, were held to have done so. R. Chanina says to the angel of Death, 'Bring me the Book of the Law, and see whether there is anything written in it which I have not kept.' (Schoettg. i. pp. 160, 161. See also Edersheim, 'L. and T.' i. p. 336).—"Alfred Plummer, Com. on Luke xviii, 21 (p. 423).

10. Cf. A. C. Headlam, "St. Paul and Christianity" 1913, p. 138. "The Reformation Controversy was really the old controversy of Faith and Works. Practically (however much it might be concealed in theory) the medieval system taught salvation by works."

11. Kostlin, "Theology of Luther," E. T. i. 479.

12. A. T. Jorgensen, *Theol. Stud. und Krit.* 1910, 83 pp. 63-82; cf. *Jahresbericht for* 1910, 1912, p. 590.

13. Kostlin, ii. 301: "I do not know any book of mine that is right, unless perhaps, *De Servo Arbitrio* and the Catechism." This was written in 1537.

13a. "The Necessity of Reforming the Church," in "Tracts," E. T. p. 134. This was written in 1544.

14. p. 159.

15. The statement as to the true doctrine of the will involved in this last sentence, is noteworthy.

16. Cf. Jean Barnaud, *Pierre Viret,* 1911, p. 505: "Bolsec, who was the first to raise himself against it [the doctrine of the Reformers] began by contesting that divine election was taught by the Scriptures, and then proclaimed the universality of grace, and, attacking Calvinistic determinism, denied that the fall had entirely deprived man of his free will. From these premises, he concluded that faith, with men, results from the exercise of free will, wounded and corrupted, but not absolutely destroyed and made incapable of doing the good, and consequently that election does not precede faith, and that salvation, finally, finds its supreme cause not only in the will of God but in a free determination of man."

17. See E. F. Fischer, *Melanchthons Lehre von d. Bekehrung. Eine Studie zum Entwickelung der Ansicht Melanchthons uber Monergismus und Synergismus.* 1905.

18. For what follows see E. Bohl, *Beitrage zur Geschichte der Reformation in Oesterreich* p. 26ff.

19. Schweitzer, *Centraldogmen,* i. p. 503.

20. p. 509.

21. *Loci*, 1610, ed. Preuss, ii., p. 866.

22. Kostlin, i., p. 326.

23. *Christliche Dogmatik,* ii., 1898, p. 146.

24. On the other hand even Th. Haring "The Christian Faith," E. T. 1913. p. 347, says, "Any suspicion that our God may be a good but impotent will, a moral genius without being master of the world, destroys the roots of all religious power."

25. p. 311.

26. p. 312.

27. p. 317.

28. p. 317.

29. p. 431.

30. p. 431.

31. A. S. Martin, art. "Election," in Hastings' "Encyc. of Religion and Ethics." V. 1912. p. 261a.

32. "The Authority of Christ." 1906, p. 140.

33. p. 143.

34. p. 349.

35. Similarly, Lewis F. Stearns, "Present Day Theology," 1890, p. 416, declares roundly: "The only power that can tear a soul away from Christ is that soul's own free will." This is as strong an assertion as possible that the soul's own free will can tear the soul away from Christ. And from that we must infer, if we may trust Rom. viii, 39, that free will is not a created thing, and indeed, to speak the truth (Rom. viii, 38), that it has no existence, whether actual or prospective. If our free will is stronger than Christ's hold upon us it is omnipotent, for he is omnipotent, and no one could be saved.

36. p. 300.

37. p. 370.

38. A. S. Martin, as cited p. 261: "The belief of the bulk of the Christian Church in all ages, that man's destiny is in his own hands."

39. *Religion innerhalb der Grenzen der blossen Vernunft (Gesammelte Schriften,* 1907, vi. p. 45).

40. Do.

41. E. Schader, *Uber das Wesen des Christentums und seine modernen Darstellungen,* 1904, quoted by A. Schlatter, *Beitrage z. Forderung d. christ. Theologie,* 1904, p. 39.

42. William Temple in "Foundations," 1913, p. 237.

43. Do. p. 256.

44. "Morning by Morning," p. 14.

45. George Tyrrell, who had his own experiences, exclaims: "Peace is more necessary even than Sacraments, which men can give and take away at pleasure, and use as a whip." ("Life," by Miss Petre, ii. p. 305). No words could better show Tyrrell's emancipation.

46. "An Answer to my Lord of Winchester's Book," 1547, in "Early Writings of Bishop Hooper," Parker Society, p. 129.

47. "That the Almighty has given it a charter, like an insurance company, of a monopoly of salvation in this portion of the Universe, and agreed to keep his hands off—"as Mr. Winston Churchill not unaptly puts it ("The Inside of the Cup," p. 8).

48. "The Rule of Faith," 1912, pp. 240ff. Cf. what is said of the Church in the Romish system by H. Bavinck, *Het Christendom,* 1912, pp. 33, 36: "All this superabundant grace (and truth) Christ has committed to his Church for distribution. In it he himself continues to live on earth; it is the perpetuation of his incarnation; in the Mass he repeats in an unbloody manner his sacrifice on the cross; through the priest he communicates his grace in the sacraments; through the infallible mouth of the Pope he leads his Church into the truth. The Church is this, above everything, the institute of salvation, no assembly of believers or communion of saints, but in the first place a supernatural institute established by God in order to preserve and distribute here on earth the saving benefits of grace and truth. Whatever may be lacking to believers in doctrine and life, the Church abides the same, for it has its center in the priesthood and sacraments and in them remains partaker everlastingly of the attributes of unity and holiness, of catholicity and apostolicity" (p. 33). "The Church alone can break the power of the seduction (of the devil and his angels), and it does that in the most manifest ways, by its sacraments and sacramentation, by holy actions (blessings, benedictions, exorcisms) and by holy things (amulets, phylacteries, scapularies, etc.); so long as the natural is not hallowed by the Church, it remains profane and of lower rank" (p. 36).

49. Conc. Trid. Sess. xxii, ch. 2.

50. We do not pause to inquire how far, in the modern Romish system, the Pope has absorbed into himself the functions of the Church, and become, as George Tyrrell would say, in a separate capacity, the representative and substitute of Christ on earth. Cf. the "Joint Pastoral of the English Catholic Hierarchy" of Dec. 29, 1900, and the controversy which arose from it, a good brief account of which is given by Miss Petre, in her "Life of Tyrrell," vol. ii, ch. vii, pp. 146-161.

51. *Symbolik*, pp. 332, 333.

52. Conc. Trid. Sess. vii, Proem.

53. Op cit., p. 244.

54. p. 274.

55. "His Divine Majesty," London, 1897, p. 191ff.

56. Dr. J. Armitage Robinson has taught modern Anglicans to translate Eph. i, 23: "The Church is the completion of Him who all in all is being fulfilled": and those of sacerdotal tendency have not been slow to utilize this understanding of the text in its entirety. Cf. W. Temple in "Foundations," 1912, pp. 340, 359.

57. W. J. Knox Little, "Sacerdotalism." 1894, pp. 46, 47.

58. "Outlines of Christian Dogma," 1900, pp. 107, 123.

59. p. 149.

60. A. G. Mortimer, "Catholic Faith and Practice," 1897, i, pp. 65, 82, 84, 100, 114, 120, 122, 127, cf. 130.

61. Cf. p. 130: "By the Incarnation and Atonement of Christ, human nature as a whole was taken into God and as a whole was saved. But"—As if there could be any "but" after this!

62. Query: Is there any such thing as the "race" apart from the individuals which constitute the race? How could the Incarnation and Atonement affect the "race" and leave the individuals which constitute the race untouched?

63. Title of a volume of Lutheran polemics by the late Dr. C. P. Krauth.

64. E. F. Karl Muller, *Die Bekenntnischriften der reformirten Kirche,* 1903, p. 451.

64a. Samuel Huber, born 1547, died 1624, Professor at Wittenburg 1592-1595, was the standard example of a "holopraedestinarian" for the next age. But the relevant teaching of this "embittered martyr of universalism" seems to have begun only in connection with the Mumpelgart Colloquy (1586). A good account of him may be found in A. Schweitzer, *Die protestantischen*

Centraldogmen, 1854, i, pp. 501ff; see also G. Muller's article in Herzog. An edition of Luther's *De Servo Arbitrio* was published at Neustadt in the Palatinate in 1591, as a weapon against the New-Pelagian notion that God had elected all men equally and has no particular election for the individuals. Luthardt speaks of the party opposed as Neo-Lutherans (*Die Lehre vom freien Willen,* C. E. Luthardt, 1863, p. 122, note). How the matter is dealt with by the Seventeenth Century dogmaticians may be seen in Hollaz, *Exam. Theolog. Acroma.* 1741, p. 643, or in Quenstedt, *Theologia Didactico-Polemica,* 1715, ii, p. 72. Quenstedt tells us that Sebastian Castalio was the architect of the error of universal election and was followed by Samuel Huber, who absurdly taught that "Election is universal, that God chose all men really, properly and unambiguously to salvation, without any regard to faith." He adds that Huber had no followers and that his error was extinct.

65. Edinburgh, 1904, p. 282.

66. London and New York, 1912, pp. 310-313.

67. "The Homiletical Review," Feb., 1910, vol. lix, no. 2, p. 101.

68. *Neue Kirchliche Zeitschrift,* 1900, xi, p. 500.

69. p. 601.

70. Schmid, p. 421.

71. As cited, p. 601.

71a. This is testified to in an interesting way by J. W. Powell, "What Is a Christian?" 1915, pp. 144-145. Deserting the Arminianism in which he was bred for Modernism—or, as he himself puts it, the Epistle to the Romans for the Parable of the Prodigal Son—Mr. Powell yet sees that he has not, as a former Arminian, really changed his position. The Original Sin and Universal Grace of Arminianism were purely theoretical, and had no bearing on active life—"theological machinery, which was the tribute paid to the literal interpretation of the New Testament." All that he has lost in giving it up, and coming to the rationalistic position of the native goodness of man, is, he truly says, "a considerable amount of obscure theological reasoning."

72. "System of Christian Doctrine," 1903, p. 417.

73. H. F. Henderson, "The Religious Controversies of Scotland," 1905, p. 187; cf. W. B. Selbie, "The Life of Andrew Martin," Fairbairn, 1914, p. 8.

74. H. F. Henderson, as cited, pp. 182, 183.

75. "Life After Death," pp. 184, 185.

76. *Grundrids af den System. Theologi,* pp. 114, 115, (as cited by Dahle).

77. "The Methodist Review," (N.Y.), for July, 1909.

78. Erlangen Edition of Works, xlix, p. 343.

79. W. P. Paterson, as cited, p. 375; referring to A. Ritschl, "Justification and Reconciliation," E. T., p. 130.

80. Erlangen Edition of Works, xviii, p. 20.

81. It is important to observe that the terms Supralapsarian, Sub- (or Infra-) lapsarian concern the place relatively to the decree of the fall given to the decree of election. A habit has grown up among historians who do not comprehend the matter, of defining Supralapsarianism as the view which holds that God's decree in general is formed before the fall. Thus Th. Haring, "The Christian Faith," E. T., 1912, p. 479, speaks of a view being called Supralapsarianism because it makes "the will of God include the fall of the first man." That the "will of God includes the fall of the first man," no Calvinist (be he Supralapsarian, Sublapsarian, Post-redemptionist, Amyraldian, Pajonist), either doubts or can doubt. No Theist, clear in his theism, can doubt it.

82. Accordingly the tendency to erect the fewness of the saved into a dogma has no connection with Calvinism as such, but is just as prominent among (for example) the Lutherans. Quenstedt, *Theologia Didactico-Polemica,* 1715, ii, p. 30, makes the first attribute of the "elect" to be "fewness," as of the "reprobate" to be "multitudinousness"; and John Gerhard, *Loci Theologici* Ed. Cotta, 1781, xx, p. 518, declares of the "object of eternal life" among human beings, first of all, that they are "few." See further "The Lutheran Church Review" for January, 1915, article "Are there few to be saved?" For hints of the Sacerdotal point of view, see F. W. Farrar, "Eternal Hope," 1878, pp. 90ff., and "Mercy and Judgment," 1881, pp. 137-155.

83. Cf. what is said by R. A. Knox, "Some Loose Stones," 1913, pp. 111 sq. William Temple has said strikingly in "Foundations": "The earth will in all probability be inhabitable for myriads of years yet. We are the primitive Church." R. A. Knox takes exception to this (which nevertheless seems true enough), and proceeds to argue that there is no solid ground for supposing that Christianity shall ever be triumphant over her enemies. "Theologically," he asserts, "it seems certain that if free will is to be more than a name, the possibility must remain open that the majority of the world will reject the Christian revelation." Certainly we agree that if the matter is to be hung upon free will there can be no ground to expect that there is ever to be a saved world.

84. Accordingly the testimony of even a Th. Haring ("The Christian Faith," E. T., 1913, p. 474) is true: "It is only through faith in the living God that faith in an ultimate goal to be surely reached has become a power in the world and in the individual heart."